Few gamekeepers are better qualified than Norman Mursell, with fifty years' experience behind him, to write about the arts of his profession — rearing the birds, dealing with vermin, exciting and dangerous encounters with poachers, working with dogs, and so on — but Come Dawn, Come Dusk is much more than a gamekeeper's manual. It carries the unmistakeable authenticity of the countryman writing about the countryside he knows and loves, and painting a picture in which its wildlife, its farming, its customs, characters and crafts all take their place. The effect is greatly enhanced by Rodger McPhail's delightful drawings.

COME DAWN, COME DUSK

Fifty Years a Gamekeeper

COME DAWN, COME DUSK

Fifty Years a Gamekeeper

Norman Mursell

Illustrated by Rodger McPhail

London
UNWIN PAPERBACKS
Boston   Sydney

First published in Great Britain by George Allen & Unwin 1981
First published by Unwin Paperbacks 1983
Re-issued 1985

UNWIN ® PAPERBACKS
40 Museum Street, London WC1A 1LU, UK

Unwin Paperbacks
Park Lane, Hemel Hempstead, Herts HP2 4TE, UK

George Allen & Unwin Australia Pty Ltd
8 Napier Street, North Sydney, NSW 2060, Australia

© Norman Mursell, 1981, 1983
Line illustrations © Rodger McPhail, 1981, 1983

ISBN 0 04 799027 9

Set in 11 on 12 point Caslon by Alan Sutton, Gloucester
and printed in Great Britain
by Guernsey Press Co. Ltd, Guernsey, Channel Islands

Foreword

by His Grace the Duke of Westminster

This book, written by Norman, encompasses fifty remarkable years at Eaton with my family. It records reflections, observations and above all a deep understanding of the infrastructure of country life which over these many years has been rocked by the rapid advancement of modern technology, ideals and values. These changes are clearly identified in the book with sympathy and understanding.

The rural community relies largely upon the stability of its people and this is a story of one such person. It is a story that I have no hesitation in recommending to you and in doing so it gives me an opportunity to record my family's deep gratitude and appreciation for Norman's life's work here at Eaton.

Westminster

1

My grandfather was an Isle of Wight man, born in the early nineteenth century, and spent a large proportion of his time in what for those days was a common occupation – smuggling. When I was a lad he told me many tales of his youth on the Isle of Wight, of how they avoided the Customs men and of the ways they disposed of their loot. He even showed me some earthenware bottles in which they carried brandy or wine under the bottom of their boats. Often, on approaching the Island, these bottles were dropped overboard tied to a line with a marker of cork, to be picked up later on a legitimate fishing expedition.

My grandfather lived to be almost a hundred years old and in fact broke several ribs while rowing a boat at ninety-seven. Probably his tales served me well in later years when I came to deal with the poaching fraternity, cousins to the old smugglers.

My father like all the family was a seafaring man and travelled the world, mainly on the larger yachts around the turn of the century. After serving Sir Thomas Lipton on several of the *Shamrocks* in Sir Thomas' unsuccessful attempts to regain the America's Cup, he became Chief Steward on a yacht owned by the 2nd Duke of Westminster and could tell many tales of the Duke's generosity and sense of humour as well as his eccentricity.

There was the time when the yacht *Cutty Sark* with His Grace and party aboard were fishing in the Arctic Circle at Bosskop,

Norway. Salmon were none too plentiful that season in the land of the midnight sun and the Duke, being at most times an impatient man, came back from a trip up the fjord without catching a fish. Although several of the party were still ashore, he sent for the Captain, a Commander Mack, and gave instructions to sail for Rock Ferry (Birkenhead), a trip of over 1,000 miles. There was a car waiting to take the Duke to Eaton Hall, his Cheshire country seat. He did not set foot in the Hall but went straight to the private golf course. His clubs were brought out and nine holes were played. Straight back to the car, Rock Ferry, the *Cutty Sark* and away back to Norway, not setting foot in the Hall at all. He did not have a companion, just played the nine holes alone.

The guests left at Bosskop had in the meantime been catching fish; the Duke had arranged local accommodation for them. In due course he rejoined them and not a word was said about his absence of several days.

At the same place, Bosskop, there was an invalid villager whom the Duke often saw on his trips as the invalid's friends would carry him to a seat on the quay when the weather was pleasant. The Duke would have a chat with the poor fellow, talking more than likely about the fishing prospects, and one day he sent for the Captain and gave instructions that an invalid carriage should be sent over for the invalid's use. A cable was to be sent immediately, but on second thoughts the Duke said, "Make it two carriages. One may break down and in an out of the way place like this it could take months to replace it." Such was the generosity and humanity of the 2nd Duke of Westminster.

I was destined to go to sea like all the family, and it was arranged that I should join the Cunard Line. But as a child I suffered from bronchitis most winters, and when I left school the doctors advised me against going to sea. As I had met the Duke on several occasions when the *Cutty Sark* was either at Cowes or lying in Southampton Water, His Grace was aware of what my future was intended to be and at about the time I was due to leave school, the summer of 1929, His Grace asked my father about me. On being told of the changed circumstances, he said, "Send him to Eaton. Basil Kerr, the Agent, will find something for him to do."

Shortly after this conversation Major Kerr was on the *Cutty Sark* for a cruise and of course the matter of my employment was discussed. I had always been interested in nature and, like most lads those days, had a considerable collection of birds' eggs. (What a good thing this has now gone out of fashion, and is in fact illegal.) Because of this Major Kerr thought it would be a good thing if I went up to Eaton and joined the gamekeepers, who in

2

those days were personal servants and to a very large degree the elite of estate employees – today, many a gamekeeper is just another worker on an estate. It was arranged that I should move to Eaton early in October 1929 after lodging and other arrangements had been made, and so my lifetime's service to the Grosvenor family began.

Arriving in Chester by train one early October afternoon was in itself an experience for me, the trains and the bustling traffic on broad, well-lit streets being a great contrast to sleepy seaside villages on the Isle of Wight. Staying at a hotel close to the station seemed out of this world, and in a way rather frightening to a lad of only fifteen.

The next day dawned chilly and overcast, but a taxi was called for the journey to the Eaton Estate. After we had left the beautiful city of Chester, with its "Rows" and ancient Roman walls, it was soon open country, and after about four miles the lodge to Eaton Park itself came in sight. The lodge-keeper on duty was dressed in the Grosvenor livery, at that time black frock coat with orange lapels, and top hat with cockade. Past the lodge we went, and on through a magnificent park full of mature trees of all descriptions.

Then the Hall itself came in sight, although only the back entrance. Standing high above all the buildings could be seen the Clock Tower, and beneath it the private chapel. The Hall itself was a magnificent building, Gothic in character and vast in proportions. Large numbers of servants were needed to run and maintain it, and there were plumbers, cabinet-makers, painters and electricians on the permanent staff. Outside, the gardens and pleasure gardens extended to nearly a hundred acres and needed over thirty gardeners to keep them in perfect condition. The greenhouses covered several acres and were full of exotic blooms and plants, with one greenhouse devoted to orchids alone.

The servants' hall was a very large room with plenty of comfortable chairs – just as well since there were around fifty indoor staff. The Head Keeper, Dick Starks, was waiting in the servants' hall and told me that he would have to go, as His Grace was going out after snipe. He would call back for me after lunch and take me to my lodgings. Around mid-afternoon he returned to the Hall and said the Estate bus would be available shortly and would take us to my lodgings on the edge of the Estate. By now the weather had changed for the worse with heavy snow falling, which to a southerner like myself was rather unusual as it was only October. Dick and I set off in the bus and after travelling what seemed miles along the Estate drives arrived at a lodge which was occupied by a Mr Jones. This was to be my new home.

3

Dick helped unload the bags and then turned to the driver and said, "'Ee be off home, lad. I'll walk." He came into the lodge and, after a cup of tea and telling me what to do the next day, set off to walk at least three miles back to his house – and that after a long day's snipe shooting with His Grace. Dick was that sort of man, who would rather walk himself than keep the bus driver waiting in the cold, although I would not be a bit surprised if there was some other reason for his long walk – maybe the chance of surprising poachers, or maybe an opportunity to see what pheasants were roosting in the area.

The wage I was to receive was the princely sum of a pound a week, paid monthly, out of which board and lodging amounted to fifteen shillings per week, so in effect a pound a month was all there was to spend! However, a pound in 1929 went quite a long way and seemed enough for my needs.

On Dick's instructions I was to walk up the drive from the lodge the following day, starting at 8 am, until I met the other keepers and woodmen, who were going to be "driving in". Driving in really amounted to driving the outlying woods so that any game present was sent towards the home coverts. This was a regular task during the shooting season, as I was to find out later.

After breakfast I went outside and could see the drive stretching away in the distance. More snow had fallen and there was a sharp frost. The trees were laden with snow and the yew bushes at the side of the drive, dipping low under the weight, formed a tunnel of silence. Setting off up the drive was like walking in wonderland. After about a mile I could see people standing about. Some twenty men were there, a few with guns but most with sticks. Dick had also arrived and introduced me. I discovered that the men with guns were either keepers or tenant farmers. Nobody seemed too happy about the weather and I soon discovered the reason when we set off to drive the woods. Several men went forward, mostly the farmers, to stand at the end of the wood, and the rest formed a line across the wood. At a signal from Dick everyone moved forward, keeping as far as possible in a straight line. Dick kept shouting at the men to "Keep in line there" and "Beatee ee bushes", to ensure that as much game as possible was put up and sent forward towards the home coverts.

By now I knew the reason why the men weren't so keen on what seemed a wonderful morning. The snow got everywhere – in your boots, down your neck and even up your sleeves. It had started to thaw, and hitting the bushes caused snow to fall in huge lumps. All the same, everyone seemed to be in a good humour.

Soon shots could be heard in front of us as rabbits were put up

4

by the beaters and the guns in the line, mostly the keepers, tried to shoot them. The rabbits made difficult targets, bobbing in and out of the bushes and disappearing under snow-covered shrubs, but quite a number were killed and retrieved by the dogs. Each keeper had a dog and a game bag, in which the rabbits were carried. Near the end of this particular length of drive-side wood, with the dogs very busy hunting through the cover, pheasants started to get up, mostly going forward in front of the beaters. One came back and in a flash, Dick threw his gun to his shoulder and brought the handsome cock-bird crashing to the ground. It all looked so simple and easy but I found out later that it took a lot of practice, a good eye and quick reflexes to shoot under those conditions. That particular type of shot, I was told, was a "snap shot", probably the most accurate but only after a lot of experience. After taking the dead cock pheasant from his handsome black Labrador, Dick gave it to me to carry – the first pheasant I handled at Eaton.

The shooting ahead of us died out but still the odd pheasant went forward, ignored by the guns in front as long as it was making for the home woods. On reaching the end of this wood everyone gathered on the drive and Dick started asking questions of the men who had stood in front: "How many birds gone forward?" "Any woodcock?" "Did 'ee see a fox?" The answers to all these questions would give him very useful information. A horse and float driven by Dick's son, Togo, came down the drive, the rabbits and pheasants were put on the float and more cartridges were issued ready for the next drive.

After the next length of wood there was a short stop for sandwiches, then off again, gradually getting nearer to Eaton Park itself which was the objective for that day. During the last drive in the afternoon a woodcock was put up and one of the guns in front killed it. The bird fell in some thick cover and it was some time before it was eventually retrieved by one of the keepers' spaniels. Dick wanted it immediately and called me to him, spreading a wing out to show me the pin feather. This feather apparently used to be in big demand by artists, being very fine and soft, but on this occasion Dick needed it for another reason. Pulling the fine feather out of each wing, he placed them carefully in a matchbox. Apparently the 2nd Duke was in the process of making a firescreen covered with these woodcock feathers – a lifetime's task, I should imagine. I wonder if it was ever completed?

There was a cottage hidden in the trees at the end of the wood we had just driven, and that was where I was to be at daybreak the next morning, to go with one of the keepers on his rounds feeding the pheasants. I set off to be at the appointed place in good time, the drive looking quite different on a damp and overcast morning to the frostiness of the previous day. As I arrived at the keeper's cottage the dogs greeted me with a chorus of barks and yaps but soon the keeper, Fred Milton, appeared and the dogs went quiet. Fred was a heavily built man who, like his father, had worked on the Estate all his life. As I was to find out, he had a mischievous sense of humour and a fondness for practical jokes, but he was an efficient and tireless keeper. No-one could have wished for a better tutor.

After a welcome cup of tea by a roaring fire in Fred's kitchen we set off across the fields and parkland to a large wood. All around the wood pheasants could be seen pecking under the oak trees. The early morning sunlight glinted on the brilliant plumage of the cock-birds, but I had to strain my eyes to pick out the duller hen-birds which were almost invisible until they moved.

Fred started whistling softly and told me to keep close to him. Soon there was a trail of pheasants following us, and after some distance we came to a hut partly hidden in the wood. Fred unlocked the hut, and inside were numerous sacks of feed for the birds. Filling a bag with about half a hundredweight of wheat and maize, Fred set off down the wood, whistling softly all the while. Pheasants came from all directions and soon the track seemed unable to accommodate another bird; but when Fred came back and I said there must be a thousand there he said, "Nay, lad, it's a poor feed this morning," so I wondered what a good feed would be like.

After watching the birds feeding for a while, Fred said that our next task in the daily routine was to look at the tunnel traps. These were gin traps set in tunnels man-made with pipes, bricks or other available material, or in holes in trees, or in drainage pipes. They are set for ground predators such as stoats, weasels and rats. This morning, after looking at several traps, Fred took a stoat out of one trap set at the base of a tree, and to my surprise cut the tail off! He explained that most keepers were paid a bonus, or "vermin money", on what predators they killed; the tails or heads were counted once a year and the keeper paid accordingly. The tails and heads were also nailed to the "keeper's gibbet", a practice now long past.

Having cut off the stoat's tail, Fred then cut a small twig about four inches long out of an adjacent bush. He split one end and inserted the stoat's tail, telling me that it was the best way to ensure that the tail didn't work its way through the pocket and into the jacket lining. Tails have a nasty habit of doing this, as I found out when a rat's tail worked its way into the collar of my coat – a rather uncomfortable position, but my fault!

There was nothing more in the traps that morning so we made our way across the fields and through a wood until we came to a long drive, one and a half miles dead straight with woods on either side. In the distance could be seen the Hall itself, partly obscured by a large obelisk. Crossing the drive and going through the wood on the other side, we came to a large house with numerous out-buildings. This was the Kennels, the Head Keeper's home and headquarters for the keepers, where we were to meet this morning. In the gun room with its blazing log fire were several keepers I had seen before, but after a while one or two more arrived, strangers to me. Dick appeared and it was soon known what was afoot that day. It was driving in again, but from a different direction, and a number of "pits" or ponds were to be included. Apparently His Grace was due back at Eaton and it was essential that there should be some snipe in the game larder; His Grace being very partial to snipe, it was the custom to keep some readily available when he was in residence.

Moving off from the Kennels, the keepers split into pairs and made off in slightly different directions. I was instructed to go with Fred. Soon we came to a pit. Pits, or "marl pits", are very common throughout Cheshire, originating from the time when farmers dug large holes to get the marl to spread on the land. When full of water and surrounded by herbage they are a favourite haunt of wildfowl. As we spread out and approached the pit from different directions, Fred made a queer noise, "Ssh-ssh", a poor imitation of the snipe's call. Any snipe that had settled on the pit

overnight soon rose and, zig-zagging away with their unusual flight, became targets for the guns. After going across country for a considerable distance we all met at the end of what appeared to be a long narrow wood. Dick asked how many snipe had been bagged and decided we had enough.

Woodmen appeared after a while, but different men from the day before. Apparently there were gangs of woodmen on each section of the Estate, and each gang joined the keepers when driving in was to take place on their patch. Once again the aim was to send as many pheasants as possible back to their home coverts. This procedure went on for about three weeks except Saturdays and Sundays and in all that time only twice was the same ground covered, which indicates the vastness of the Estate.

One day after I had been at Eaton about ten days Dick said, "'Ee come with I to Chester today, lad," so off we set in a pony and trap. Arriving on the outskirts of the city, Dick went into a pub yard and handed the horse and trap over to a man in the yard, telling him we would be away about an hour. Only now did I know the reason for my journey into Chester: the tailor's, to be measured for a suit and to be supplied with other accessories The suit — jacket, waistcoat and breeches — was made of a very hard-wearing, dark grey material which everyone called "pepper and salt", and to be worn with it on "ceremonial" occasions were a hard hat ("blocker") and fawn box-cloth leggings. These suits were supplied every year, usually during the summer months, but the tailor promised Dick that all would be ready in ten days' time so that I would be presentable and not stick out like a sore thumb when the shooting days started.

With the last week-end in November came the start of the shooting season proper. The 2nd Duke never shot pheasant until then, although the season officially began on 1 October. With the leaves off the trees and the birds really mature, it made for much better shooting. Stronger birds tend to fly faster and higher, which was a very important factor in pre-war days. Shooting was to take place on two days, Friday and Saturday, and as the weather had settled down to clear days with just a slight breeze and plenty of birds coming to feed, the omens were good. Dick himself seemed eager and excited.

A few days before the shoot, Fred took me to put the pegs out on his beat. These pegs, white-painted stakes numbered from one to twelve, marked the positions the guns were to take before the beaters drove the wood to send the pheasants over them. Fred explained to me that the guns would stand at some distance from the wood, in a position where the pheasants would come over at a maximum height. They were spaced out approximately forty yards apart, and if the required number could not be put in one row the remaining pegs were put further back, between those in the front row. It was interesting to see the trouble taken to get the pegs in the right spot and to make sure they were an equal distance apart. It was important that the numbers could be seen when facing the wood being driven; the guns stood with the numbered pegs in front of them and by tradition the rows always numbered from right to left.

Fred also went round all the gates in the area through which the guests might have to pass and made sure that they opened easily. Gates were well maintained in those days and seldom needed any attention before a shoot, but a check was always made just in case.

On the Thursday before the shoot, a conference was held in the gun room at the Kennels and each keeper involved in the next day's shooting was given instructions by Dick. I had to be at the Kennels before daybreak and Dick would take me with him until the guests arrived. After that I was to go to Fred Milton, carry cartridges for him and make myself generally useful; Fred always acted as His Grace's loader, and I have never seen anyone more efficient or safe when handling a gun. I was looking forward to this, my first big shoot.

Friday turned out to be a lovely autumn morning and proudly I put on my new suit which had arrived from the tailors as promised. On arriving at the Kennels, I found Dick already about. I hardly recognised him! He was dressed in the livery of a Head Keeper and looked very impressive in green velvet jacket and waistcoat with white breeches, box-cloth leggings and a hard hat with plenty of gold braid around it. Of course the brass buttons on the jacket and waistcoat really shone! He said it was time to go and as dawn was breaking we walked up the drive to the Hall. Groups of men were standing around there, chatting expectantly. But as soon as Dick shouted, "Right, let's 'ave 'ee, lads," they all lined up like soldiers on parade. There were over eighty men and lads present, all dressed in the same rig-out: a red, wide-brimmed hat with a leather band, and a white smock made of a very rough material in the "Farmer Giles" style and gathered in at the waist by a wide leather belt with a large brass buckle. The legs were adorned with strong, brown, leather leggings. There was a variety of footwear, as wellington boots were not readily available in those days and in any case probably cost more than one week's wages.

Dick walked among the row of beaters as the other keepers looked on. He chatted to one or two, mostly the older ones who were by all accounts semi-retired but just had to turn out on a shooting day for the pleasure they got out of it. Dick also inspected the lads very thoroughly and drew the attention of one to the condition of the brass buckle on his belt which was not well enough polished. Above the leafless trees the sun rose on the beaters in their red and white, all assembled in front of the "Golden Gates" and in the background the Hall, with lights still shining through the many windows.

When the time came to move off, each keeper took the number of beaters allotted to him. Their job was to make sure that as many pheasants as possible were in the woods to be driven that day. Also, a certain number of the beaters would be placed out as "stops" so that once the birds were in the woods they did not have the opportunity to come out into the fields and hedgerows again. The whole operation was a complicated one and the beaters had to know the terrain well; after driving the birds into the woods they would meet up at a given point, ready to drive the first wood and send the pheasants over the guns for the first stand of the day.

With the keepers and beaters on their way, Dick took me with him to the Hall itself. There at the servants' entrance were gathered a number of men, most of them wearing breeches and leggings. Some I recognised as farmers who had been driving in with us during the previous weeks. They were busy loading leather boxes containing cartridges onto a horse-drawn float, each magazine having its owner's name engraved on it and in some cases a crest as well. There were also shooting sticks, cartridge bags and other items. Dick took me to this float and pointed out which things belonged to His Grace. He told me that I should probably need to refill the cartridge bags after each stand but Fred would give me instructions about that.

After everything was loaded onto the float, it was driven away by Togo, Dick's son, and I saw it next at the end of a wood which was the first stand. Shortly the bus, an old-style version of the modern mini-bus, arrived. This vehicle was known all over the area as the "Eaton bus" and was used as a fetch-and-carry transport. Now it was filled to capacity with at least twenty men and lads aboard and many pairs of guns. It was the responsibility of the loaders to look after the guests' guns and to make sure that they were not damaged or maltreated in any way. Even in those far-off days guns were extremely expensive, and those on the bus that morning were the best that money could buy.

The shooting was due to start at 9.45 am and to be late was unthinkable. Driving away from the Hall, the bus took us about a mile down one of the drives to a wood called the "Young Wood", a name which must have been given to it when it was first planted.

10

Now part of it is being felled, but I don't doubt it will still be called the "Young Wood" in the twenty-first century! The float was waiting with its load of cartridges and impedimenta and soon the loaders were sorting out the cartridge bags and coats of the gentlemen they were loading for. The loader retained one cartridge bag, while the lad who was carrying for him was handed two bags each containing 200 cartridges, with a coat or two and probably a shooting stick.

Fred gave me His Grace's supply of cartridges and so on, and when everyone was loaded up the float departed. All the loaders and lads waited on the drive-side and during the wait Fred told me what I must do and what I must certainly not do. One thing I remember was that on no account must I put anything on the ground, no matter how heavy it became – and two bags of cartridges, 400 cartridges in all, became very heavy after a very short while!

Shortly before 9.45 am several cars appeared, a Rolls-Royce, a Daimler and one or two more large cars, all chauffeur-driven. His Grace stepped out of the Rolls and soon all the guests were assembled and passing the time of day with the waiting loaders. Fred told me to hand His Grace his shooting stick as on this occasion His Grace did not have his "crumbick", a long walking stick with a forked top as a thumb-hold. The Duke led the way along the drive until the first numbered peg was reached, then turned round and told one of his guests to take his position there. The loader and lad of course stopped with him. His Grace walked the full length of the pegs putting a guest on each one as he came to it and taking the last peg for himself. This he often did, as it ensured that his guests got the best of the shooting and also left him in a position to see how they performed. It was normal for the guns to draw for position before the day's sport began, but the Duke very often spoilt the usual procedure of then moving up two places at each stand by taking up whichever peg he fancied – usually an end peg or one in the back row.

As soon as His Grace got to his peg Fred blew a whistle and an answering whistle could be heard in the distance; it was Dick starting the beaters off in the wood. Within minutes shooting started, and it built up to a barrage as the pheasants came out of the wood in a steady stream. I was of course fascinated by all the birds and all the shooting, but by now His Grace himself had started shooting and Fred was fully occupied, handing him a loaded gun and reloading the one he had just fired. The pheasants were falling like autumn leaves, and to me it was a never-to-be-forgotten occasion. I stood and watched Fred changing guns with the Duke

11

with incredible speed, and never was His Grace waiting for a gun, or a target for that matter. The shooting went on for quite half an hour, one continual bang, bang, bang, building up at times almost to deafening point. In the rare moments of comparative silence the tap, tap, tap, of the beaters' sticks could be heard in the distance, and sometimes a muffled voice. The red and white of the beaters' garb eventually appeared through the bushes and the stand came to an end.

Now more men appeared from behind where the guns had been standing. They all had dogs, some two or three. The duty of the "dog men" was to make sure that all the pheasants that had been shot were picked up and that any wounded birds were quickly despatched. No doubt some of the birds had only been wounded but the bulk of those I had seen fall had been killed cleanly, through the heads. I was impressed by so many things at that first stand, the first I had ever seen, but I think the quality of the shooting stands out in my mind, the style of gun handling that is rarely seen today. The loaders, too, were most impressive and of course were a very important part of the proceedings. It was rare indeed for one of the guests to be without a gun in his hands when a pheasant appeared, and the speed at which an empty gun was changed for a loaded one had to be seen to be believed. Quite two hundred cartridges were used by each gun during this rise alone, in the space of thirty minutes or so — not much hanging about in those days!

As soon as the guns had finished shooting the car in which they had arrived appeared, followed by the Eaton bus. The guns in the cars and the loaders in the bus, we all arrived eventually at a large wood behind Dick's house, the "Kennel Wood", and at once took up positions on the now familiar pegs. This time Dick had travelled with the loaders, and as soon as all were in position he blew his whistle. Almost at once pheasants started to come over the guns, and once again a barrage of shots rang out as the birds hit the ground in ever-increasing numbers. This rise lasted about the same length of time as the first one — I later learnt that thirty minutes was about the average time for most stands at Eaton. It appeared that half of the beaters had been in position on our arrival at the Kennel Wood, so that the shooting could start immediately the guns were in position. Meanwhile the beaters from the Young Wood had come across country and were ready for the next drive, the last before lunch.

The 2nd Duke was very impatient at times, so all efforts were made to cut to a minimum the time that guests had to wait before shooting started. This was why so many beaters were required. One party of beaters had often partly driven a wood to get the birds in the right position for flushing, while in the meantime other beaters had moved to the next drive to await the guns, and they usually started beating when the shooting stopped at the previous stand. It was all organised to the fine degree that was essential to provide the sport which His Grace wanted and expected.

After the third drive of the morning there was a break for lunch, when His Grace and his guests went back to the Hall and no doubt were served a sumptuous lunch by the staff on duty. The loaders, keepers and dog men went to the gun room at the Kennels and used the stables and outbuildings as a resting place to have their sandwiches, hotpot and even slices of a large game pie, all to be washed down with ale drawn from a barrel in an adjoining room. Dick was hovering around, making sure that one and all had whatever they fancied, and also making sure that the keepers' lads carried enough jugs of ale to the beaters to quench their thirst. I remember the ale was drunk from horn jugs. I wonder what has happened to those?

After about an hour it was time to move and this time we walked a short distance across the drive to a wood called the "Brickyard". The guns had not arrived, of course, but after a short while a rumble was heard from the direction of the drive, and lo and behold the private narrow-gauge train was coming from the direction of the Hall. It was pulling passenger carriages, all brightly painted in the Grosvenor colours, and stopped as close as possible to the Brickyard. The passengers started to dismount, and this time the guests had the ladies with them. Etiquette laid down that the ladies did not appear until after lunch, and this was strictly adhered to until the Second World War intervened and changed so many things.

The guns once again took up their positions, and soon the shooting was fast and furious. Two more stands took place during the afternoon, both within walking distance of the Brickyard, and each one produced just as much shooting. When the last drive had taken place, with the sun setting over the Welsh mountains to the west, the keepers came out of the wood but the beaters remained in a line at the edge. As the guns departed His Grace made a point of thanking each keeper individually as he made his way to the train, waiting to take the shooting party back to the Hall. Nowadays, I'm sorry to say, the beaters often run, yes, run from the wood as soon as the shooting has ceased. So many of the so-called "beaters" of today only do the job for the money, with no real interest in the day's sport.

The loaders and cartridge-carriers made their way to Eaton and the gun room. Dick told me to stop with him and I watched as the last of the day's bag was loaded onto the game cart. This ornate, horse-drawn vehicle had been following the proceedings all day. It was a wonderful sight in itself, the horse brasses gleaming and the intricate patterns of the paintwork recently varnished. When laden with the day's bag it was something never to be forgotten. It could carry about a thousand pheasants, all hung by the neck in the correct manner.

Dick then took me to the Hall to join the loaders, who had by now cleaned the guests' guns and got everything ready for the next day's shooting. The keepers soon arrived after hanging the pheasants in the larder, and this was a sign for the glasses of whisky to appear. There was talk of the next day's shooting, which was to take place on a different part of the vast Estate, and much leg-pulling about who was loading for the best shot.

It is impossible to assess accurately the number of birds killed until they are hanging in the game larder, so everyone was waiting for the arrival of the man in charge of the game cart, a retired Regimental Sergeant-Major whose responsibility it was to count the heads once all were hung in the larder. The morning's bag had been hung up at lunchtime, so the afternoon total had to be added and the grand total reported to Dick at the Eaton gun room. "Major" Potter eventually arrived with his slip of paper and

14

handed it to Dick, who announced the bag for the day. With the passing of time I cannot remember the exact figure, but it was certainly very close to two thousand, about the usual number for the first day's shoot at Eaton fifty years ago. Dick went off to see His Grace's private secretary who was still on duty. The total bag had to be typed onto a special game card, which had the Grosvenor crest on the front and inside the names of the guns shooting, the beats shot over and the number killed. These cards were placed on the dinner table that night, one for each guest.

The next day, Saturday, the proceedings were as before but on an area which I had not seen before. One drive in particular stands out in my memory, the "Torment". The pheasants were driven over some very tall elm trees and provided the most difficult shots, testing the skill of even the top-notchers. This drive is still used today, but thanks to the loss of the elms with Dutch elm disease and only a comparatively small number of pheasants, cannot be compared with the pre-war days. By the end of the day, with four drives in the morning and three in the afternoon, the total bag was not far off the previous day; His Grace was pleased that his guests had had two days' good sport, and the keepers were pleased to see a satisfactory result from all their labours.

During the rest of the winter two more two-day shoots were held, followed by a day when cock-birds only were killed. This killing of cock-birds only on the last day was to ensure that there would be enough hens for stock for the following season. Now I was to find out that the real work to provide good shooting was about to start.

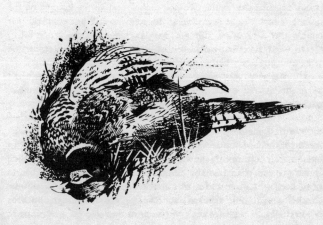

2

When the shooting of game ends the work begins. Every keeper will agree with this, but before the war even more work was involved. So it was after my first winter at Eaton. The Estate in those days was divided almost in half by the River Dee, each half providing one day in the two-day shoots, and all the keepers on the northern half would assemble at the Kennels at 9 am each day. Of course the day's work did not start at that time: the keepers had already fed several points, probably as many as ten, getting the pheasants together before catching them for the laying pen.

The priority now was to get the large pens ready to take the pheasants as they were caught. About four acres near the Kennels, partly rough grass and partly shrubs and trees, were permanently fenced in with wire netting. This netting, which was seven feet high with a one-yard cross-piece on the top, had to be checked inch by inch throughout as even one broken mesh would present an opening for any fox in the vicinity. The cross-piece on top, which was a protection against any climbing fox – yes, some can – had to be at the right angle and firmly attached. All these things had to be checked and double-checked, and the ravages of weather and time repaired. Dick Starks was as particular as ever and even set some of the keepers to rake up the pockets of leaves under the trees and burn them. This, I found out, was to make it easier to find the eggs when the laying season came in April. Then the water troughs had to be cleared out and some of them re-sited. Although Dick did not actually work at any of these tasks himself, he often came to see that all was going as it should.

Seven or eight men and lads worked for more than a week on the two pens into which the four-acre area was divided. At last all was ready for a start to be made on catching the pheasants. Each pen was of a size to hold five hundred hen-birds plus a cock-bird to each six hens, so almost twelve hundred pheasants had to be caught. In practice it amounted to more because not every bird caught was suitable for stock. The cock-birds in particular had to be carefully selected and some hens were also rejected for various reasons: hens too small or damaged in any way were useless for breeding purposes.

Now Fred Milton had me with him most of the time. He it was who showed me how to position and erect the wire cages which were the main method of catching pheasants in those days. Take about five yards of three-feet wide, two-inch-mesh wire netting, and peg it to the ground in the shape of a heart. The "vee" in the heart is the entrance tunnel for the birds, and of course the top is folded over to create a cage from which they cannot escape. Fred explained all this to me, and told me he always used long, thin sticks to interlace the join at the top of the cage. This makes it much easier to take any pheasants out that have ventured into the trap. These cages are fed and wheat thrown around the area for a week or more, with the wire lifted off the ground so that the pheasants have a free run and get used to the presence of wire netting.

As soon as the laying pens were prepared, the catching of the stock birds began. The usual practice is to "set" the cages, that is to peg the wire firmly to the ground, shortly after dusk. The reason for doing this after dusk is to save any birds being in the trap overnight: a pheasant confined to a small wire cage soon becomes the victim of Reynard. It also makes such a mess of the cage, with feathers everywhere, that there is little hope of catching more birds without re-siting the trap.

Going through the twilit woods with Fred to "set up" was rather an eerie experience, with the odd owl hooting and the trees taking on unfamiliar shapes in the gathering gloom. Fred knew every inch of his beat, though, and walked as sure-footedly as in daylight; the task of pegging the traps down, with some wheat in the middle and just a trickle in the tunnel, was soon done.

About mid-morning the next day we visited all the traps to

collect the catch. Some had seven or eight birds in and others only the odd one, but all were put into sack bags and carried to Fred's hut, to be collected by horse and float and taken to the laying pens at the Kennels. The afternoon was spent putting the pheasants into those pens. Every bird was carefully examined and any that were suspect were rejected and later released into the woods. Each one that was retained had a wing tied with tape to prevent it from flying out of the pen. This is called "brailing", but today leather or plastic brails are used and are much easier to put on. Two men are needed for the tape method but the leather brails can be put on single-handed, which speeds up the handling of the birds.

With each beat keeper bringing in fifty or so birds each day it was surprising how soon the pens were full. The same thing was going on on the other half of the Estate at Aldford, so when the job was done around two thousand hens were in the pens, ready to produce the eggs for the coming rearing season. These penned pheasants were fed on good-quality wheat twice a day, morning and night. One feed would probably have been enough but would have meant food lying about most of the time, which would have attracted all sorts of unwanted visitors – rooks, jackdaws, rats, mice – which would have been a menace when the pheasants started to lay.

Dick detailed two keepers to be responsible for the laying pens, and to share the load different keepers were allotted this task each year. One of the two detailed for my first season was Fred, so of course I was involved.

About mid-March the feed was changed from dry wheat and a boiler came into use. The boiler was half filled with water, the wheat put in when the water was hot, and the whole thing boiled until the wheat had swollen and absorbed all the water. This boiled wheat was fed to the birds after being dried off with barley meal and "laying meal", a meal made up of maize and oats with spices added to encourage them to lay.

Today the stock birds are usually retained from the rearing pens. This makes for a small amount of extra work during the shooting season, since any birds in a pen need regular feeding, but saves most of the task of catching. Also, it makes it less important to leave hen-birds at the last shoot. Although it must help to a certain degree to have hen-birds on the Estate at the end of the shooting season, in Cheshire they rarely have much success in rearing a brood. Being mainly a grass county as opposed to arable, Cheshire is a very "hungry" place as far as game is concerned, and with several packs of foxhounds hunting the county, foxes abound.

There have been vast changes in the methods of egg production since the war. In the mid-1950s Eaton changed from the large, open laying pens to smaller, twenty feet by ten feet pens. With the use of hoppers for the feed, this made life much easier. The large open pens needed someone on hand throughout the laying period as carrion crows would appear from nowhere, snatch an egg and be gone in no time at all. Vigilance was essential. In the smaller pens a wire netting roof protected the eggs, making constant attendance unnecessary. On some shoots the large pens are still in use, since I suppose the cost of lost eggs and keepers' time has to be set against the cost of providing smaller pens, but in my experience the small pens win hands down. Apart from releasing the keeper for other tasks, there is only one cock-bird in each pen with seven hens and fertility is certainly higher, a big advantage. This is probably because there is no fighting between the cocks. Modern compound feeds also make the use of a boiler obsolete, turkey breeders' pellets being most commonly used. With a hopper holding up to three weeks' supply of food, only a fresh supply of drinking water is needed, and regular collection of the eggs. Such are the results of progress.

Many shoots now buy either the eggs from game farms or day-old chicks. This saves you the trouble of catching and penning pheasants for your own egg production, but you do not know what type of birds you are going to get. There also seems to be a growing tendency to buy in six-week-old birds, poults, but again the quality is to say the least rather doubtful. There are so many different strains of pheasant today that it is almost impossible to get, for instance, a pure-bred "Mongolian"; when buying in you are liable to get anything from a "cream" to a black "melanistic". I suppose in a lot of cases this is of no great importance, but it has been proved at Eaton that one strain is much more satisfactory than a "mixed bag".

For many years the old English Blackneck type (I say type because, although most of the cock-birds have black necks, odd ones do appear with a semblance of a white collar) has been the strain used at Eaton. The terrain is pretty flat but despite this the Blackneck, if handled properly, can provide some excellent shooting. It is very handy, lays an excellent number of eggs per bird and when mature is only an ounce or so below the average dead weight of about three pounds, so it is also good for the table. On top of that, if the retaining and catching of stock is done properly the Blackneck appears to be less inclined to stray than many other types.

It is now the custom at Eaton to keep all hen-birds required for stock penned from the poult stage, but the cock-birds are caught up

19

at the end of the shooting season. These cock-birds are caught from the "home covert", that is the wood where they have been reared and released the previous summer. They are carefully selected, any with the slightest sign of a white feather being rejected. The reason for taking the birds from the home covert is simple: any bird that has survived a winter's shooting, been driven over the guns probably half a dozen times, and more than likely chivvied about by the foxhounds more than once, is pretty obviously a "stay at home" breed if it is still at the point of release. All pheasants have an inbuilt tendency to stray but with a little care this can be reduced to a certain extent.

But way back in 1930, other essential duties were still being carried out at the same time as catching the pheasants for the pen. Setting the cages was so arranged that Wednesday was left free, at least Wednesday afternoon. One Wednesday in February Dick Starks said to me, "'Ee come with me tonight, lad," and told me I was to see some pigeon shooting. In those days there were literally thousands of pigeon roosting in the woods during the winter months, and these destructive pests can provide some very good sport.

About mid-afternoon we set off for a very large wood called the "Duck Wood". As the name implies, there was plenty of water there. The wood was about ninety acres of mature timber, mostly oak, and divided at about twenty-yard intervals by wide drainage ditches, each with planks crossing it at frequent intervals. This wood was a favourite roost for pigeon: being on low ground it was well sheltered, and about a mile and a half to the south there was a vast area of market gardening with plenty of winter greens, brussels sprouts, spring cabbage etc – marvellous feed for the ever-hungry pigeon.

At this wood we found several men waiting, strangers to me, but Dick introduced them. One I remember was the gunsmith from Chester, whom I later came to know well, there was the local police sergeant and several shopkeepers from the city – Wednesday was chosen because it was early-closing day in Chester. All the woods on the Estate had their quota of guns, mostly the local farmers but also a number of people interested in shooting and glad of a shot. This was more than likely the only time of the year that some of them were able to take the gun out, yet they were quite good shots.

They had all been pigeon shooting in the Duck Wood before, and Dick told each of them which position to take up, and suggested that they might be able to shoot a carrion crow or two if they remained in place for a while after the pigeons stopped coming to roost. We moved off and Dick chose to stand by a large oak, on the side from which a slight breeze was blowing. He told me that pigeons nearly always come to roost into the wind, so by taking up that position he was less likely to be seen. Also the birds would be going-away targets for him and so it was more likely that the shot would penetrate under the feathers. Because of the density of a pigeon's feathers, an approaching bird needed to be quite a bit closer to the man shooting.

Soon the pigeon began to arrive in hordes. The sound of shooting could be heard coming from distant woods where other parties were also after pigeon, and Dick soon had his first shot. He was using a most effective sixteen-bore hammerless gun. He could really handle it, getting several right-and-lefts. During any lull in the shooting he sent me to pick up the birds shot down, and soon there was quite a pile — I could see pigeon falling out of the sky, shot by the other guns, but the birds just flew round and then kept coming back into the wood. The barrage continued for the best part of an hour but, as the light faded, it died away to just the odd shot.

Dick said he wouldn't wait for the crows to come to roost that night so, gathering up the unfortunate birds, we moved out of the wood. We waited for some of the other pigeon shooters to come out, as Dick wanted to get an idea of how they had fared. Several soon appeared and all had a heavy load of pigeons. The exact number I cannot remember but they all seemed very pleased with the evening's sport. They were of course allowed to keep what pigeons they had killed, and no doubt pigeon pie would be on the menu in many a household during the next few days.

I do remember that Dick had started the evening with three boxes of twenty-five cartridges each, and the number of pigeons he had accounted for totalled seventy. He said there should be seventy-one since he had missed only four and told me, I must admit politely, that I had failed to pick one up. On the Thursday morning he sent me to see if I could find the other pigeon that he was sure he had killed. I reached the Duck Wood, but lost my bearings in the maze of ditches and planks that had to be crossed and re-crossed. I could not find the position Dick had taken up the evening before. A number of pigeon feathers lying around the base of one tree made me think I had found it, but on getting closer I saw that the empty cartridge cases heaped against the tree were twelve-bore not sixteen. After further searching I eventually found the right spot and the empty cartridge cases of a sixteen. Despite looking high and low I failed to find another pigeon, but I did find a carrion crow which must have been killed by one of the guns

21

which had remained behind. A pigeon was not to be found, though, so rather disappointed, I made my way out of the Duck Wood.

For some unknown reason the empty cartridge boxes which Dick had pushed into a rabbit hole the previous evening seemed to be uppermost in my mind. I pulled them out of the hole, one box rattled – and lo and behold, there was an unused cartridge! Full of a sense of achievement, I made my way back to the Kennels. Soon Dick appeared and asked, "Did 'ee find it, lad?" When I produced the cartridge he examined it and said, "That be one of mine." After hearing where I had found it he chuckled, "Be your turn to cuss me now!"

Many hundreds of pigeon must have been killed during the four Wednesdays devoted to the job way back in the 1930s. Many people had a lot of fine shooting, but I doubt if really much good was done in reducing the number of birds. Year after year as many as ever came to the winter roosts and nearly every wood on the Estate was full of them. Some say vast numbers crossed the North Sea from Norway and Sweden – no matter, they still did as much damage to farmers' crops. At the same time they provided a good cheap meal for the country folk. Since the very severe winter of 1963 there do not seem to be so many of the pigeon flocks about. It would be a good evening's pigeon shooting now if one gun bagged twenty or so, and it is pretty certain that six guns in the Duck Wood would not get as many as Dick shot that first night I went with him. It may be different in some parts of the country but Cheshire is certainly not plagued as much as in the past. There may

be a smaller amount of market gardening but in all there must be much more arable land. In autumn the countryside is a patchwork quilt of green and gold, and a large proportion of the green growing is winter wheat and barley, which should provide plenty of young greenery for the pigeons during the winter.

Many seasons of pigeon shooting have passed since I first went to the Duck Wood with Dick, and up to 1963's hard winter most years were pretty good from the shooter's point of view, if not the farmer's. Clover crops and any winter greens all suffered, kale being a particular favourite, and if the grey hordes were left undisturbed they would soon reduce this valuable farm crop to nothing but stalks. On one occasion pigeon were devastating a field of kale on the Home Farm, so of course the keepers put the birds on the move whenever possible. Once I was passing this field and could see one mass of pigeons, perched all over the kale and all busy filling their crops before going to roost. (A pigeon with a crop full of feed must be almost double the weight of one with an empty crop, so goodness knows the weight of food devoured by a flock of probably eight hundred to a thousand birds!) I was approaching from an angle which gave me an opportunity to get within range of the feeding birds without disturbing them, so decided to see what two barrels from a twelve-bore could make of them. Closing to within about forty yards, I fired one shot into the crowd of feeding birds and, as they arose in alarm, fired the other barrel into the flying birds. It appeared to rain pigeons, with a cloud of feathers drifting off in the gentle breeze. Amazed at the number of pigeon that fell, I searched the kale for some time and discovered that I had picked up thirty-three birds – not bad for two cartridges! The range from which I had shot at them was probably a big factor: too close (most unlikely with feeding pigeon) and the pattern of shot would not have spread enough, too far and the penetration of the shot would not have been great enough. On that particular occasion the range must have been just about right.

Some episodes of pigeon shooting always remain in your memory. Again this was in the Duck Wood, but on this expedition I was with another keeper, George Astbury. Pigeons were plentiful, as usual pre-war, but it had been rather a wet winter and the Duck Wood was partially flooded. The raised planks crossing the ditches were visible, but the greater part of the wood was under about six inches of water. Still, we were young and not really bothered about the conditions, and we knew that Duck Wood would be shunned by most people. We were wearing waders, so had good hopes of plenty of sport.

It was no problem getting into our places in the daylight, and

23

the numbers of pigeon that came in were fantastic. Having eventually run out of cartridges and picked up as many of the birds brought down as possible – no easy task splashing about in six inches of water, with hidden deep ditches – I made my careful way to where I knew George was standing. He saw me coming, or more likely heard my splashing progress, and shouted to me to wait, he would come to me and we would go the shortest way to dry land. About thirty yards away from me he had to cross a wide, deep ditch by means of a plank, obviously not very level, with only about a third of it showing out of the water on George's side. He started to cross, laden with pigeons – a game bag full to capacity, both hands full and some tied in a bunch over his shoulder – plus a gun under his arm. He did very well until he was halfway across the water-covered part of the plank. One more step, there was a great splash and all I could see were the barrels of a gun above the water and masses of dead pigeon bobbing up and down! I know it could have been dangerous, but to me at that moment it was hilarious. George had disappeared completely. After a moment – it seemed ages at the time – his hand holding the gun appeared, then his head, and soon he was sitting on the part of the plank out of the water, giving vent to his feelings on his misfortune.

We never did know exactly how many pigeon were bagged that day, as we had to leave quite a number floating about in the Duck Wood flood water. It was one of those afternoons never to be forgotten, but not really one you want to repeat.

The lads in the Game Department were always ready for the chance of a shot, so pigeon shooting time was very popular with them. Dick was generous with his issue of cartridges, taking the view that without practice there was no chance of becoming a good shot. The lads made sure that they got that practice! In pre-war days a keeper had to be able to shoot well for, as well as killing vermin, there were many times when game of all descriptions had to be obtained for the larder at the Hall.

One cold, blustery night I went pigeon shooting in a wood called "Speeds Wood". Snow was in the air and after we were in position it started to fall. Tom Starks, one of Dick's sons who was with me, shouted to say we were sure to have a good night. We did! The harder it snowed the more pigeon came in flying very low, battling their way through the snow. We had some great sport but the snow was getting deeper and deeper and in the strong wind the trees soon became white. In the by now deep snow it was difficult to find the pigeons we had shot, but no matter – to us the sport was the main thing. Eventually the time came to leave, but on arriving at the spot where we had left our cycles, we found

them completely buried under a snow drift. Getting onto the main road was a real task, with snow drifting up to two feet deep. The cycles had to be carried and with pigeons and gun made quite a load with which to battle through the blizzard. That was one night's pigeon shooting from which we were glad to get home!

Another time I recall wasn't a pigeon shooting night, but quite a few pigeons were killed nevertheless. A large number of magpies had taken to roosting in a wood called the "Fox Covert", and in order to reduce the numbers I decided to wait for them to come in at dusk. Several of the magpies were shot, then there came a lull; no doubt the rest were sitting in trees outside the wood, undecided what to do. During this lull the pigeon came in in droves, and a lot settled in a young ash about thirty feet high near my position under some spruce trees. I stood watching as the boughs became literally covered, with not a space for another bird. It was too much, I just had to shoot. Up with the gun, bang, and it just rained pigeons. Eventually I returned twenty-two birds, all from a single shot. I think you can call that economy of cartridge!

The type of wood makes a lot of difference to the type of pigeon shooting. An old, mature, mixed wood offers the most sporting shot as a rule, but as it is more open, you often find less pigeons using it as a roosting place. Of course the guns are more easily seen by the incoming birds, which often take evasive action, and this in itself gives a more difficult target but a really sporting shot. So the number of birds killed in a mixed wood is often smaller, but oh, what fun! The younger plantations, such as those of the Forestry

Commission, are usually of softwood species like spruce or larch, which as a rule give a dense canopy. These woods are much loved for roosts by pigeon, and an experienced shot in the right position can get quite good bags. The shooting itself is not so interesting, as the birds coming in are often unaware that a gun is waiting for them.

That very severe winter of 1963 thinned the pigeon out dramatically. To start with, the guns were out in full force in the market garden county, but as the weeks passed it was no longer necessary to shoot the birds. The damage was done: what the pigeon hadn't devoured, the severe frost finished off. The birds became so weak that it was possible to walk into a field of any green crop and kill them with a stick. Of course the farmers took advantage of this, and one used a tractor and trailer towards the end of the winter to remove the carcasses and bury them.

Cheshire at least has never seen the same number of birds since, even during a frosty spell of weather. Small numbers do come of course, and at the proper time some pigeon shooting is done. Some woods are favoured more than others as roosts, but even in a "good" wood, not many of the sportsmen go home with more than ten birds. Fewer people in any case turn out to shoot pigeon these days – the price of cartridges? Pre-war there were so many pigeon that anyone invited to come pigeon shooting all four weeks that it took place would go to the same spot each Wednesday. Now, to give the guns a fair chance it is arranged for each of them to go to a different wood each week that shooting takes place.

The farmers should be pleased about this decline in numbers, but I've noticed that pigeons seem to visit the cottage gardens more than they used to. Some of them in fact have become quite tame and cheeky – but not in my garden!

* * * * *

Dick Starks was a strict, kind and helpful Head Keeper. During my first six months at Eaton he took me with him most of the time and explained everything that was going on and why. From the time of my arrival in October a large number of rabbits were being killed every week on driving in days, but as soon as the stock birds had been caught and penned a real onslaught was made on them. Rabbits were to be seen everywhere, literally thousands of them, so it was essential that they were drastically reduced before they started to breed in the spring, because such a vast number of them could do a great deal of damage to both farmland and young

plantations. In those days all the keepers kept ferrets, which now had to earn their keep.

I did not go with them ferreting that first season, but the custom was for the keepers to work in pairs on a given area, and to kill as many "conies" as possible. In woodland, it was usual first to drive the wood, shooting as many as possible and of course making quite a lot of them go to ground. Around the park at Eaton the land is clay, so the rabbit burrows are not very deep. This made it much easier to ferret, or at least dig out. Once as many rabbits as possible had been put to ground ferreting started, and in those days it was quite a bit of fun. It was quite usual for two keepers to kill two to three hundred rabbits a day. This was where I became involved that first season. Dick used to go around with the horse and float during the early afternoon to collect the rabbits from the keepers, leaving them to carry to the Kennels any killed after his visit, and of course I went with him. After picking up the rabbits from three or sometimes four gangs, the float was pretty full. The rabbits were all taken to the game larder at the Kennels and hung up, ready for the keepers to "paunch" (take the insides out) when they returned.

After a week's rabbiting it was not unusual for the game larder to be full, maybe two or three thousand rabbits. Nearly all of these were sold, many of them going to Liverpool and Manchester, but the keepers could always have a few to give to anyone who might have proved helpful in any way. A couple of rabbits made a very acceptable gift in those days, especially where there was a large family.

Many ways of killing rabbits were employed. In the parkland where large numbers of rabbits were sitting out in rough cover rather than living underground, it was usual to snare them. Snares set correctly could account for many of these "outlying" rabbits. Most snares were hand-made by the keepers themselves, using thin brass wire and very often the "lines" (cord) out of old "long nets". It was possible to tell by the way the snare pegs had been trimmed who had made them, which was very helpful as it made it easy to

27

know if poachers had been trying their luck! About a hundred snares were the usual number in a line, and on a good night could easily account for sixty to seventy rabbits. Snaring is a great art: you have to know how to read the run used by the rabbit, and how to assess the correct place to set the snare by the size and shape of the pad marks. The height of the pear-shaped loop from the ground, and its size, are important.

Weather also plays a great part in a good catch. When rain is threatening, rabbits tend to feed heavily and so are less cautious travelling to their feeding point, being in a hurry to feed. A moonlit night is not very good for snaring rabbits, particularly if new snares are being used. The brass wire, reflecting the moon's light, makes the rabbit shy off, so on a light night old, weathered snares are usually more successful. Some operators used to smoke the wire by holding it over a candle or other smoky flame, but the real experts always had a good supply of weathered snares for use in all conditions. In my experience the smoking trick was not too successful as the discolouration was often rubbed off whilst the snare was being set or washed off should it rain.

At one time there was an outcry about the use of snares – they were cruel and far from humane. The result was a so-called "humane" snare, actually a snare with a knot in it. With the coming of myxomatosis and the wiping out of almost the entire rabbit population, little more was heard of the humane snare but, in any case, the plain snare if expertly used was probably more humane than the knotted variety. Correctly set, a snare catches the rabbit in front of the ears and only one jump by the victim is needed to break the neck. As with so many things when dealing with nature, it is the experience and practice which make the essential tasks humane.

Trapping was another essential part of the effort to control the pre-war plague of conies. Trapping seldom took place at Eaton

Park, but the other side of the Estate at Aldford, where the soil is very sandy and the rabbit burrows large and deep — warrens in some places, in fact — trapping was the most successful way of dealing with Bunny. Gin traps were used, now of course illegal, and trapping involved a large amount of work. The custom was to use one gross (144) of traps to each gang of trappers, and to have two gangs operating, one from each end of the beat. The traps were left in the same burrows for six days and then moved forward, until after about four weeks the entire beat had been trapped. Setting the traps and securely stopping all the holes was a laborious job, not too pleasant on a cold or wet day. Of course these traps had to be looked at night and morning, and the catch taken out and traps re-set, and any holes that had been opened up re-stopped. When the beat had been trapped once it was usual to repeat the process, but this was easier as the traps covered a larger area and there were less holes to stop.

By and large this was a cruel method of dealing with rabbits, some of them remaining underground for several days before facing the gin trap. By that time they would be quite thin and very often useless as food. I am not sorry that it is illegal to use that type of trap, and certainly at Eaton trapping no longer takes place.

Dick Starks was very keen on controlling the rabbits and on one occasion he was instrumental in my old friend George Astbury and myself taking on a bet thrown out by the Head Forester, Sandy Myles, that George and I wouldn't kill twelve hundred rabbits in a week. It appeared that an area was to be planted with young trees, so the less rabbits around the better — it is amazing the number of saplings that rabbits can ruin even though there appears to be plenty of feed available. We agreed so long as the week was seven days. The wager was to be for a bottle of whisky, valued at twelve shillings and sixpence in those days.

George and I planned out the best way to approach our task and eventually decided to snare as wide an area as the rabbit runs would allow and then ferret as much as possible, shooting the rabbits in order to save time digging out. Fortunately cartridges were readily available so there were no problems in that respect. We also decided that should we fall behind schedule day by day some "long netting" would help to keep us on target.

Starting early one Monday morning with each of us setting snares, we got off to a good start and with ferreting throughout the day managed to reach our required number by the following Friday afternoon. This really does give some indication of the vast numbers of rabbits in the countryside during the 1930s. Those rabbits were killed in just one small area — which in a way, I suppose, made it easier for George and myself to claim Sandy Myles' bottle of whisky.

One occasion which sticks vividly in my mind was a November day during the mid-1930s. There had been a few days of quite heavy rain, and the River Dee duly responded to the influx of water from the Welsh hills. This particular day His Grace (the 2nd Duke) had been snipe shooting round the marl pits and I was in attendance. At that time George Astbury was driver to the Game Department, which was the only Estate department to have a car, apart of course from the Duke's. On our journey back from the snipe shooting we had to cross the river via the "Iron Bridge". Fred Milton (the Duke's loader) said, "Pull up, George, let's have a look at the river." The river was rising rapidly and rushing under the bridge with great force, carrying all sorts of debris with it, even large tree trunks. A large flood was obviously imminent, and Fred remarked, "It will wash all those rabbits away at the Crook-o-Dee, but will save us a job."

After unloading the car at the Kennels, George said, "Let's go and look at the Crook-o-Dee." I should explain that the Crook-o-Dee is where the river takes a large sweep round, causing a horseshoe-shaped meadow of about ninety acres; when the river starts to flood it cuts the corner off, leaving an island. When we arrived at the meadow the river was just trickling across, and along the banks could be seen numerous rabbits which had been flooded out by the rising river. This was too much for us, and starting off one each way round the horseshoe, we soon came across some rather panic-stricken conies which were easily despatched with a stick. When we eventually met up, we had as many as we could carry in comfort. Getting them back to the car, we came to the conclusion that the water was not rising too fast, as we had only four or five inches to wade through to get to the "island". We decided to do another journey round, as it would be a shame in the end to see so many rabbits swept away and lost. So off we went, and this time there seemed to be more conies about. The water was reaching higher up and further into the river-bank burrows. Rabbits were everywhere, even running in front of us almost like a flock of sheep.

Eventually we met, once again laden with rabbits, and it was only then that we realised that the river was considerably higher. Back across the meadow was a vast expanse of water, but so intent had we been on our task that the water had risen completely unnoticed. It was no use, we had to get back and fast, but despite the obvious danger we didn't dump our load. Before long we found ourselves paddling through water seeping over the bank, and

within fifty yards of safety found the water deeper and deeper, rising almost to our knees. With still some distance to go we had to climb onto the rail of the meadow fence. Edging our way across and keeping some distance apart, we found the flood water pouring onto the meadow with terrific force. At the deepest part the water was lapping the top rail of the fence but the Lord was with us, and despite being wet through we still had our rabbits when we did make landfall!

It was a never-to-be-forgotten experience, and we were lucky not to be swept away by the rapidly rising flood water. Looking back across the meadow once we had recovered from our exertions, we could see that the post-and-rail fence was completely submerged for at least forty yards, and very little of the field left dry. Never since have I seen the river rise so quickly and with such force. In fact, when the water eventually subsided the fence had been uprooted and a large section had disappeared, carried down-river and probably out to sea. I remember this incident so vividly that the number of rabbits that we hung in the game larder will never be forgotten — it was eighty-four.

The next day, telling our experience in the gun room at the Kennels brought us both a real ticking off for being so foolhardy. It was an experience, but we weren't too keen on going after rabbits after that if there was a flooding river involved!

Throughout the country in those pre-war days rabbits created a lot of work, many men being fully employed on rabbit control alone, and of course in earlier times rabbits were bred as a crop and were penned in a warren with a full-time warrener to look after them. Today they appear to be on the increase again despite the regular outbreaks of myxomatosis, which although it still kills large numbers is not so devastating as the original outbreak. It is doubtful to my mind if rabbits will ever reach the vast numbers of the past. By the use of "Cymag" (a cyanide gas preparation) those involved in agriculture can deal with them in a reasonably humane way. To gas rabbits in their burrows is no doubt effective, and I suppose economically it is the best way, but so much good food is lost that it seems a great shame, while the rural scene is the worse for the loss. In my youth almost every field had its quota of the coney, and the countryside was much more attractive for that.

The farmers at Eaton were not allowed to have a day's ferreting without the presence of a gamekeeper, who usually provided the ferrets. On larger farms two keepers would attend, and it was a good day's sport for the farmer and his friends. Often they would breakfast at the farmhouse before the day's proceedings began, and at about midday lunch would be sent down the fields to the party. It was not at all unusual for two or three hundred rabbits to be shot, which kept the farm staff busy carrying them back to the farm buildings. The Christmas period was always a popular time for the smaller farms to have a day at the rabbits, making it a family affair, and the sale of rabbits – about sixpence each in those days – no doubt provided a little extra cash for the holiday.

It was the custom for the shepherd on the Home Farm to have a day's ferreting on Boxing Day. Tom Jones, the shepherd, had permission to kill the rabbits round the sheep and hen runs on the Home Farm. On one such day I was detailed to go with him and after a glass of cider the first job was to go round the runs, which were boarded up to about three feet from the ground, and stop any holes to prevent rabbits which bolted from escaping. Tom wanted

to make sure he got as many as possible, since they were one of his perks. After "entering" the ferrets, it was just a question of standing back and waiting for the rabbits to bolt. Tom was an elderly chap with a large bushy moustache, his firearm was an antique hammer gun of unknown origin, and he always wore a trilby hat with a large brim. Now, when a rabbit came to the surface and started to move around the run looking for an escape hole, Tom would stare at it, slowly tip his trilby off his forehead, wipe his moustache with the back of his hand, gently lift the hammers of his gun, take aim and fire. It had to be a patient rabbit to wait for that procedure to be completed! There was no way out for "Mr Coney", and very few escaped Tom's relentless approach, but they all had to be stationary before he would fire, determined to make every shot count.

This time, a rabbit came out but would not leave the burrow, sitting still just outside one of the holes. Tom waited some time, then decided to shoot it where it was. He went through the ritual — and the rabbit moved just as he pulled the trigger! Of course he missed it, but I saw something moving in the hole. Going up to it, I found an almost dead ferret. Tom hadn't missed! But of course he was very upset. There were several more ferrets in the box so the day proceeded, eventually finishing with quite a good bag. Tom never forgot shooting a ferret, and would not fire at another rabbit unless it was well away from the burrow.

Although quite a lot of rabbits were killed during the shooting season, the main onslaught was started after Christmas — as I said at the beginning of this chapter, the end of the season meant the beginning of the real work. I was going around a lot with Dick Starks during this time, but listening and talking to the other keepers and lads made me aware of the work and the long hours ahead. Even so, there was some relaxation: if they wanted to, the keepers could usually have a few days off during February and March, perhaps to visit relatives and friends. And at the end of March, His Grace always arranged for a coach to take a party of servants to Aintree to watch the Grand National. Of course not all his servants could go in any one year as there would be a house party of probably twenty guests at the Hall for the occasion, but each March several keepers were invited to make the trip. I was to be at Eaton for some years before I had the pleasure of that outing.

3

The approaching spring at Eaton, as everywhere, is heralded by the awakening of the countryside. One spot known as "Primrose Hill" was ablaze with pale yellow blossom at this time of the year, giving notice to one and all that spring was on its way. Alas, this pleasant area is now planted with trees but fortunately they are mixed trees, predominantly hardwoods, so maybe one day in the future, when the trees are big enough to smother the ground cover, the primrose will once again be there to welcome the warmer days.

Spring to me always means bird song. Eaton, lying as it does in the Dee Valley, still has a good quantity of both winter and summer visitors. Take the chiff-chaff – now there's a marvel of nature. A small, unobtrusive bird, it flies all the way from the Middle East to treat us to its spring song. Well, it is hardly a song, but it is nearly always the first call of a spring migrant heard in this area and to me means that the new season is almost with us. Our resident birds are not far behind in the welcome to spring, and I suppose the green plover (peewit) is one of the earliest. It usually starts in early March, but I have heard it quite early in February if the weather is particularly mild. Its rather melancholy call as it swoops and dives over water meadow, ploughed land and winter-sown corn alike is a sure sign that eggs will soon be laid in its apology for a nest. The plover normally makes several nests, shuffling around in a suitable spot to make a small dent in the ground. In one of these the well-camouflaged eggs, normally four of them, are laid. Being of a stone or bluey-green base colour with dark speckled spots, they are not easy to find.

"Bend-Or", as the 2nd Duke was so affectionately called, was very fond both of plover eggs and of entertaining on the large scale, particularly if a popular event was taking place nearby. For the Grand National house party at the end of March, just the time the plovers were starting to nest, His Grace always wanted plover eggs on the menu. (It was much later that it became illegal to take wild birds' eggs, with a few exceptions.) The keepers had to collect the delicacies, which could be a tedious job if the weather was poor as the birds were rather slow to lay. Fortunately there were very large numbers of the birds on the Estate in those days and four or five keepers, methodically walking back and to across a field or water meadow, soon became aware if eggs were available by the number of "scrapes", or false nests. Early in the season most nests had only one or two eggs, not the full clutch of four, so it was pretty certain that no incubation had taken place and the eggs were fit for eating. We usually had to get four or five eggs for each guest, so up to a hundred eggs were often needed.

One keeper, Tom Lamont, had a black labrador, called Tom too, who would quarter the field on its own and, on finding a nest with eggs, would stand with tail outstretched like a pointer. This was a great asset, and any party of plover-egging keepers always made both Toms welcome! I don't think the collecting of plover eggs made any difference to the number of chicks hatched. Being birds that normally nest early, many of their eggs are lost to predators – there being very little ground cover in March – or even to a late frost or now and again by the water meadows becoming flooded.

As the weeks passed the activity of the keepers increased and I was now spending all my time with the "gang" rather than with Dick Starks. Various jobs needed the full staff to cope with them quickly. Several days in March were spent in cleaning and lime-washing the coops to be used on the pheasant-rearing field. About eight hundred were used in the Park and a similar number at Aldford, which always provided the second day of the two-day shoots and was run more or less independently. Each coop had to be checked to see if it was still sound, before being brushed, scraped clean and lime-washed. Any needing repair were put on one side for the Estate joiners. The lime-wash was always made from lump lime soaked in water, which created heat and was in those days a more or less effective way – in fact about the only way – of disinfecting the coops. Some estates used creosote on the coops, which was also a good disinfectant as well as a preservative, but it had the disadvantage of making the inside of the coop dark, and a rather dismal, dreary place for a broody hen and chicks. At least the white lime kept it light even if it had no preservative value.

At the end of March Dick Starks told me that I was to spend every third day with his son, Togo, who was in charge of the pheasant pens that year with his mate, Fred Grass. My job was to attend to the boiling of the feed in the morning and to wash out and refill the water containers — it was important that good clean water was always at hand for the laying birds. Came the last day or two of March and the first egg was laid. I have never known penned pheasants to start laying later than the first of April. In fact even if snow is on the ground, which is not unknown on that date, the first egg is always to be found.

As the days progressed the number of eggs increased until the peak laying period was reached in early May. All the eggs were carefully checked and any cracked or misshapen ones rejected. Storing the eggs involved a good deal of work: all the eggs for hatching were placed, large end uppermost, in a specially made tray about three feet by two feet and filled with clean sawdust from the Estate yard, and every morning Togo would move the eggs so that the "germ" did not become set in one place. Any spare time during the day was spent watching the pen to ensure that no crows, rooks or other vermin raided it in search of eggs. Any that did appear had to be dealt with, but it often meant a long wait well out of sight before having a shot at them

One day when it was my turn to help at the laying pens, Togo took me with him to feed the various wildfowl in the huge gardens at Eaton. There was a great variety of ornamental fowl: mallard, pintail, mandarin, even a pair of pelicans! In addition there were a pair of monkeys on the very nice island in the Fishpond lake. All these had to be fed once a day — fruit, nuts etc for the monkeys,

fish for the pelicans and grain for the ducks. It was normally Togo's brother, Tom Starks, who did the daily feed, but Tom was away that day, hence my visit to the gardens with Togo. The grain was kept in the bin by the water, but the fruit and fish had to be collected from the kitchen at the Hall. Laden with the necessary food, we went down to the lake, where the ducks came to meet us and were no problem to feed. The pelicans were a different thing altogether; they kept their distance until a herring was produced, then they made one dive for it, but it was important to be very quick and throw the fish before the birds got close to you. Togo showed me a scar on his knuckles where he was once caught by a pelican's beak. They have a saw edge to their bills which can inflict a nasty wound.

The monkeys were not easy to feed either, or rather they were easy enough to feed but not so easy to get away from. It was the usual practice to row across to the island in the boat, throw something to the monkeys as soon as you were close enough, then step ashore and put a supply of food in the small "house" for the future use of the monkeys. The trouble was, as soon as you got back to the boat the monkeys would jump in with you, and unless you had kept an orange or two back it was most difficult to get them to leave. But throw the oranges well onto the island, and with luck you would manage to get clear while the monkeys retrieved them.

Some years after my visit to the island at feeding time with Togo, Tom, his brother, was feeding the monkeys and having trouble getting one of them to leave the boat. One of the staff was watching the performance and, having a camera with him, took a snap of the monkey sitting on the seat beside Tom. Eventually Tom was given a copy of the photo, which had come out very well, and was proud to show it to all and sundry. Weeks later Tom was again feeding the monkeys when His Grace appeared. On Tom's return to the mainland, and after some talk about the monkeys, the Duke said, "I understand you have a photograph of the monkeys, Tom." Tom was highly delighted at the Duke's interest and produced from an inside pocket a by now rather dog-eared photo. Handing it to the Duke, he said, "That's me, I'm the one with the hat on, Your Grace." I believe this incident was repeated many times over dinner at Eaton!

But back to the laying pens. As the pheasants were busy laying the eggs, preparations were in progress to hatch them. This involved taking the sitting boxes out of store and getting them ready. These boxes, each about ten feet long by one foot three inches wide, were divided into eight compartments, each large enough to hold a broody hen. One wood, the "Gullet", had a wide, sandy track which was ideal for a hatching yard. The boxes were lined out either side of this track, fifty or so each side. They had to be levelled, in a perfect line – Dick Starks would see to that! – and each section about quarter-filled with a sandy loam. The loam was shaped into a nest, which later had a lining of soft meadow hay, to accomodate the eggs and broody hen. Down the middle of the track was a treble row of forked pegs about two feet high (usually cut from elder), each peg with a looped string to which the hen was to be tethered whilst feeding.

About the middle of April was the time to collect the broody hens, and a large area had to be covered to obtain the eight hundred or so needed in the Park alone. Few cars or lorries were about in 1930, so a lot depended on horse and float. A hen-collecting expedition usually started about four in the afternoon and, whatever transport was used, the idea was to make for the furthermost point and work towards home. It is more likely that any hens still on the nest box by the late afternoon are broody, but of course the keepers were expert in telling which hen was broody by the clucking and the loss of breast feathers. The cash price paid in those days was four shillings a bird, and most farmers jumped at the chance. Later, about early September, the same birds were sold for two shillings each and would lay eggs all the winter – a good buy, especially for the cottagers.

The twentieth of April was normally the day the first batch of eggs were put under the broody hens – depending on the date of Chester Races! Most keepers liked a day at the races and plenty of free passes were available, so care was taken to ensure that the eggs were not due to hatch until after the race meeting!

The day came to put the first lot of eggs down, and Fred showed me how to slip them under the sitting hen with the minimum of disturbance. With the lid of the box closed, most hens were very snug and soon settled down, but any that was uneasy had to be changed for a more placid bird. About a hundred birds were given their clutch of twenty eggs each and another lad, Bill Rowlands, and I had the task of checking for any cracked eggs after the journey from the laying pen. A broken egg in a nest usually made the sitting bird so uneasy that the whole clutch was spoilt.

Each morning all the broodies had to be taken off the nest and tethered to the pegs to get a feed and a drink, but after fifteen minutes at the most it was back to the nest to carry on the incubation. Even working in two gangs of three, when all the sitting boxes were full we took two hours or more to complete the task. It was back-breaking work, being bent all the time, and a thankless task on a wet morning.

After twenty-three days the chicks had started to chip their way out of the eggs, and great care had to be taken when replacing a broody hen after it had been fed. On the twenty-fourth day the nests were full of lively little balls of fluff, dashing all round the box in an attempt to hide, as they would do in their natural state if disturbed.

While the collecting of eggs and broodies was in full swing, the field on which to rear the pheasants was also being prepared. As large a field as possible was necessary to accommodate all the coops needed for rearing on a large scale. For my first rearing season at Eaton the field chosen was part of the actual Park, a section that had been fenced off for many years and was known as the "Enclosure" (now part of the golf course, which was enlarged from nine to eighteen holes during the mid-1950s). It was planned to have around eight hundred coops of birds from hatching yards all over the Estate on the field, so we needed approximately eighty acres. Coops were spaced twenty yards apart each way: twelve coops per acre and each row of coops had to be as straight as a die. Dick Starks explained to me one day that nice straight lines of coops presented a more attractive view from His Grace's private golf course nearby than coops dotted anywhere. In fact coops were always "lined up" on the bird field; much more attention was given to the look of things in those far-off days, and it is a shame that so much importance is not attached to tidiness today. A tidy mind is usually an orderly one which must in the end produce the best results.

On the evening of the twenty-fourth day of incubation, the hatched pheasant chicks had to be taken to the waiting coops on the bird field. It was a wonderful sight to see a large wooden box full of several hundred lively, yellow and tan chicks, all cheeping like mad after being taken from their foster mothers. With the cuckoo calling high in the trees, yellowhammers with their "little bit of

39

bread and no cheese" call, warblers of all sorts and the distant call of the corncrake, it was a scene which, once you had experienced it, stayed with you for ever. Alas, it is doubtful if it will ever be repeated, if only because the corncrake is very rarely heard in Cheshire now.

The Gullet with its sitting boxes was just at the end of the Enclosure, so with some of us carrying the hens and others the chicks, it did not take long to transfer them. Once the chicks were settled under the hens, they were left undisturbed until the next day when they received their first feed. This feed consisted almost entirely of hard-boiled eggs which had been pressed through a sieve and mixed with barley meal. Fred Milton took me round with him on this first feed, so that I could see how much or rather how little feed was needed. It had been quite a good hatch, so Fred said: from the Gullet there were eighty-one coops full of chicks, each coop having twenty, so in effect this meant an eighty-one per cent hatch. The hens had started off with twenty eggs each, so nineteen of the broodies had sat in vain. These rejected hens found themselves in a pen specially erected for them, and after a week or so were sent to market to be sold as boiling fowl.

It was some way round eighty-odd coops twenty yards apart, but from now on it was the routine to feed them four times a day. After about two to three days, according to the weather, the chicks were allowed out of the coops and great care had to be taken not to tread on them. As they grew they needed more food, plus fresh water and grit, so this meant more journeys round the coops.

Shortly before dusk, all the coops with chicks out had to be shut up. I was soon to discover that this was an art in itself. The coops had to be approached with the greatest of caution, otherwise out would pop the chicks and the little devils wouldn't go back until they had cooled off – and on a summer's night that could be a long while. The fact that each keeper had to go back to any coop he had failed to shut up encouraged a stealthy approach!

Eventually the bird field was full of coops and the coops were full of chicks. Now each man had well over a hundred coops to feed, which meant a lot of walking. Going round them five or six times a day for six weeks must have meant a fair mileage in all weathers. A lovely morning, with the sun coming up at dawn in a clear blue sky, meant for certain very heavy dew, night and morning. On a wet day, walking through long grass most of the time could not be called a pleasant exercise. Many older keepers suffered from what they called "screw", mostly in their legs – rheumatism of some sort, I suppose. It was not unusual to get wet round the legs several times a day most days for six weeks. In the early 'thirties there was not much in the way of waterproof clothing, so there was very little choice but to get wet and often not much chance of a change of clothes either. By the outbreak of war in 1939 wellingtons were available and also waterproof slips for the legs, so – touch wood – up to now I have escaped the "screws".

"Old" Ted Milton, Fred's father, was in charge of boiling the food for the growing chicks. Ted was semi-retired but always available for odd jobs and, with his long experience, was a most useful man. I had to help him with the boiling, a rather tricky job any time. First, crates of eggs had to be boiled. They were Irish eggs, I remember, 360 to a crate, and to save time and handling the eggs were boiled in the crates! Once the water was boiling one end of a crate was put in (it was too big to fit in all at once) and the eggs cooked for about ten minutes to make sure they were hard-boiled. The crate was then turned over and the other half cooked. The usual ration was one egg per coop per day so at least two crates had to be cooked.

Once the eggs were cooked, the harder grains like buckwheat and hemp were put into the boiler, which held forty gallons. They took longer to become soft than did groats and rice, which were added later. When these were boiled until soft, the fire was withdrawn and maize grit slowly added until the whole mixture was dried off. This brew was added to biscuit meal and egg, which had been rubbed through a sieve, and there you had the feed for the birds. Later, when the chicks had grown, a dried meat called "greaves" was added and the whole lot mixed into a crumbly consistency by adding barley and bean meal.

41

That is a rough idea of the work involved just in preparing the food, but Ted Milton was a dab hand at that part of the job even though he took no part in the actual feeding of the coops. He was a stickler for cleanliness; all utensils, buckets, baths and benches had to be scrubbed in boiling water after the last feed in the evening, and of course the boiler refilled ready for the next day. Sometimes the lads would be sent out in the evening to shoot rabbits, which Ted liked to put in the feed now and then. They were skinned and boiled and the flesh put through a large mincing machine before being added to the feed instead of the dried meat. Now and again various herbs would be added to give the chicks a bit of variety, chopped spring onions and wild sage being the favourites. I don't know why it had to be wild sage but quite a lot was growing on the Estate at that time, probably encouraged by the keepers. Today I would be hard put to know where to look for this herb.

The weeks passed in what to me was a most interesting task, but the days were long. From six in the morning until eleven or later at night was a hard day, even if the weather was good. Each day brought fresh things, and there had to be constant vigilance over the vast field to ensure that vermin were not making regular raids.

That time of the year, May and June, is of course the breeding time for vermin as well as pheasants, so there are plenty of hungry mouths to be fed. Once, say, a carrion crow started visiting the pheasant rearing field, there was no peace until the unwanted intruder had been dealt with. This usually meant a tedious wait in the right spot until a quick, accurate shot saved further loss.

Winged vermin could be seen easily from quite a distance, but a sharp eye had to be kept for ground vermin such as stoat, weasel or rat. A cackling hen often indicated that something was amiss, or small birds in the hedgerows could tell you if there was mischief afoot. Stoats and weasels could be much worse than winged vermin, and even a rat could take a lot of chicks before being settled with. I have known two adjacent coops emptied of pheasants by a weasel which has popped up out of a land drain — a most difficult customer to deal with.

One occasion I shall never forget was on my first rearing field and was my first shot out of a twelve-bore. Fred had noticed that one coop near the edge of the field was losing some chicks, and watch had been kept for what appeared to be ground vermin. One feeding time I was at the cabin with Ted Milton when Fred shouted for me to bring a gun. I hurried across the field, treading warily so as not to step on any chicks. As I reached Fred, he pointed out a slight movement in the grass about five yards from the coop and told me to shoot at the spot as soon as I saw any more

movement. Apprehensive and excited, I waited. Soon there was a movement and I gingerly put the gun to my shoulder, slid the safety catch off and gently pulled the trigger. The explosion did not sound as loud as I had expected and, despite a slight kick in my shoulder, I was still in one piece. The same could not be said of what I had shot at, though, which was now a mangled mass of feathers. It had been a hen pheasant. I was horrified, but Fred explained to me that sometimes a hen pheasant will kill other pheasant chicks, maybe because she has lost her own or because she is sitting close by and becomes jealous of these unexpected neighbours. So although out of season, this poor hen bird had to be killed to save the lives of who knows how many chicks on the rearing field. That was my first shot out of a twelve-bore, the first pheasant I had killed and all under rather unusual circumstances.

After six weeks the birds first hatched were due to go to the wood. This meant an early start in the morning in order to get the job finished before the normal feeding time. At about 3.30, just before dawn, two or three of the Forestry Department's horse-drawn lorries arrived on the field. As the lorries moved down between two rows of coops, the keepers working in pairs would drag a sack under each coop and gently lift coop, hen and chicks onto the lorry, making sure that no legs were trapped. The sack was necessary because the coop had no bottom to it. Once the lorry was full, it trundled off to the wood where the coops were unloaded and the sacks withdrawn. After a couple of hours or so the now quite big pheasant chicks, called "poults" at six weeks old, were let out of the coops and fed in their new surroundings. From now on they received three feeds a day and were called to feed by the keeper in charge, usually by whistling.

Later, boxes were introduced for moving pheasants from the rearing field. These put a certain amount of stress on the young birds: as each box was divided into two sections, one for the foster mother and one for the chicks, it meant handling the occupants of every coop. But overall they made the moving of the birds to the wood much easier, as long as there were enough surplus coops to have some ready and waiting in the wood.

This method of rearing pheasants needed a lot of manpower. It was always reckoned that each keeper would rear one thousand birds to poult stage but at Eaton, with several lads and a semi-retired keeper or two, the number reared by each keeper actually doing the feeding was nearer fifteen hundred. About seventy-five per cent of chicks hatched survived to poult stage, which in the light of modern rearing methods makes pre-war rearing seem a rather hit or miss affair: in fact, to calculate the number of eggs to be put down, it was normal to put under broodies twice as many eggs as the number of six-week-olds needed.

Things have changed dramatically over the last twenty-five years and today rearing pheasants is really a simple job once the necessary equipment is available. After the death of Bend-Or, the 2nd Duke, Gerald Grosvenor took up residence on the Eaton Estate. Shooting still carried on, but a much smaller number of birds were reared than had been the case pre-war. It soon became very difficult to obtain broody hens because broodiness was being bred out of poultry, and in 1956 Colonel Grosvenor sent me to the Game Research Centre at Fordingbridge to look into the possibility of rearing under infra-red lamps. Pheasant eggs had been hatched in incubators for many years, but the larger the numbers the more the problems started to multiply. But the experiments carried out at the Game Research Station went a long way to ironing out the snags, and after my visit there it was decided to go ahead with a pilot scheme at Eaton, using incubators and brooder houses. A number of "still-air" paraffin incubators were bought second hand, over-hauled and installed in a smallish brick building. The incubators had to be levelled to ensure an even temperature over the egg trays and provision made for additional moisture in the building; humidity is critical, at least during the last four days before the hatch is due, and it was essential to be able to boost it.

Eventually, after following closely the notes I had brought back from Fordingbridge, we put the eggs on the incubator trays. They had been selected very carefully, even more carefully than when putting under broody hens. These eggs had to be turned three times a day by hand, a rather trying job. "Turning" did not actually mean completely turning the eggs, but rolling them half way round and then back to the original position at the next move; "move" is a more accurate description of the operation. After twenty-one days of being moved at 8 am, midday and 8 pm, the eggs were left alone apart from taking the tray out once a day to cool them. This corresponded to a hen pheasant going off its nest to feed!

During this period of preparation I had great support from the Game Research people and a Mr Fant, their expert on incubation, arranged to be at Eaton the day the first hatch was due. I must admit I was not too optimistic about the outcome but Mr W.A. Redfern, the Estate Agent by then, was very interested in the scheme and gave me great support throughout. Other keepers were very pessimistic, prophesying, "If you do hatch 'em you won't rear 'em, and if you do rear 'em they'll be too tame and won't fly." Time would tell.

The twenty-fourth day arrived and the chicks were appearing quite nicely on the tray in the incubator. During the afternoon of the hatching day Mr Fant arrived and took a quick peep at the hatching eggs. He advised me to leave them alone until the next morning, when he would come back and work out what percentage the hatch had turned out to be.

The next morning at 8 am was the time to open up and take the chicks out. It was an exciting moment, and with a cuckoo calling in the tree above the incubator house, a start was made on putting the chicks into the chick boxes. Two keepers, who shall be nameless, came by and when Mr Fant said, "This is the method of the future," both of them shook their heads and said it would never work. But after some quick figuring on a cigarette packet, Mr Fant announced that it was a sixty-eight per cent hatch of eggs set, which compared quite favourably with the seventy-five per cent by now being reached under broody hens. The two visiting keepers were rather impressed, and I remember Mr Fant's words to them as they left: "Go ye to breakfast, with what appetite ye may." There seemed to be no doubt that it was possible to hatch well with a still-air incubator, and that artificial incubation was the way in the future.

Once the chicks were hatched, they were left for several hours on top of the incubators to dry off properly before being taken to the brooder house which had already been prepared. There, infra-red heaters had warmed the pea gravel on the floor, and food and water were available for the incoming chicks. After three or four days the chicks were let out into a small grass run, and of course shut up again in the brooder house before the evening air became too cool. The basic principles were simple enough: as the chick grew the more room it needed and at three weeks, if the weather was right, heat was withdrawn, although shutting up at night was essential.

At six weeks the poults, as on the open pheasant field, were ready to be taken to the wood, but they had to be released in a different way. As they had no foster mother there was nothing to draw them together once they were out: no clucking hen, and of course groups of a hundred and more as against the fifteen or twenty in a coop. It was found that if a covered release pen, four yards by six with a reasonable amount of cover, was built in the wood, about a hundred poults could be released quite well. At this stage the poults were fed at three fixed times a day, so they soon got to know feed time. Once they were waiting for feed, a few could be let out of the run and after the initial shock of being in strange surroundings soon came to feed around the release pen. Usually, after a week's careful feeding the pen could be thrown open and soon all the poults were feeding happily on the feed track.

This is a brief outline of the method we were changing to in 1956, but of course it took a year or two to iron out the snags that appeared, and I like to think that our early pilot trial contributed a lot to the progress that has been made. It is pretty certain that rearing pheasants is now as easy as it is ever going to be. There are of course plenty of pitfalls to be avoided, but advice is readily available and many variations of equipment are used, from ultra-modern expensive incubators and electronic hatchers to the "pig lamp" and old hen-house!

Many of the advantages of brooder house rearing are not really appreciated. The predator problem is practically nil, there is no feed to boil and mix and no long wet grass to walk through day in

and day out. It is now quite normal to hatch seventy per cent of the eggs put in the modern, all-electric, practically automatic incubator, and really no great problem to rear ninety-plus per cent of those hatched. This must in itself be an improvement, plus the fact that one man can without much effort rear twice as many as the old-timer on the bird field.

I wonder what the old-time keepers would think of the way of things today? Many of the older keepers that I knew in the 1930s had such a fine instinct as to what was required to rear pheasants that somehow I couldn't see them approving of "them new-fangled ideas". However, change is inevitable and it is both cheaper and possibly more efficient today. On the other hand, a lot of the old skills are being lost — it is almost more important now to be a joiner and electrician than a naturalist, as most old keepers were, and the feed comes ready to use in twenty-kilogram bags! That is really the reason why birds can be reared so easily now. Modern feeds in crumb or pellet form are available with varying amounts of protein for different types of birds — pheasant, partridge, duck etc — so that instinct to give growing chicks what they need is no longer required. It is all written on the bag!

Colonel Grosvenor was very keen on the modern method and for several years very accurate figures had to be kept in order to compare costs. One day I was in the incubator house entering figures essential to the costing operation, and as usual when my pipe was drawing well, it was a bit on the foggy side. Being engrossed in the bookwork, I hadn't noticed the Colonel come in, until in his unmistakeable voice I heard, "That tobacco is a bit loud, Norman." He no doubt got the full benefit of the smoke, which I must admit was a bit strong! Being a perfect gentleman, he then offered me a pipe of his rather aromatic tobacco, which I didn't really like, but of course I was hardly in a position to refuse.

In those early days of the new method it was found that six-week-old poults could be produced at about one-third of the cost of traditional methods, by putting a ten-year depreciation on most of the equipment. After twenty-five years some of the original equipment is still in use but unfortunately would cost at least treble to replace today.

After over twenty years' experience of working with incubators and brooder houses, I find that old Ted Milton's insistence on keeping everything spotlessly clean has proved to be more important than ever. It is much easier to transmit a disease when young birds are overcrowded and believe me, once it starts it spreads like wildfire. Several, in fact many diseases were not heard of or maybe even known before the last war. Fortunately modern medicine keeps up with this, modern feeds contain beneficial supplements and others can be added if necessary. Most diseases can be dealt with if spotted in time but it needs constant vigilance.

But back to 1930. Although the poults had been transferred to the woods on the horse-drawn lorries, they needed the same dedicated attention as on the rearing field. I spent some time with the semi-retired keepers, Ted Milton, Charlie Worthington and Joe Saint, on the now quiet bird field. All the coops had to be cleaned and stored in "deersheds" ready for the next season, tunnel traps had to be removed and so did the huts used for storing the food and so on. These old hands had many a good tale to tell of their youth, which would take us back over a hundred years now! There was the time Charlie Worthington (then working on another estate) had to go to an adjacent shoot to "pick up" on a shooting day. Charlie, always rather immaculate, decided to wear a new pair of leather boots for the occasion. The journey entailed a walk of about four miles across rough country, and on arrival Charlie met the Head Keeper, who asked him how he was. Charlie replied, "My feet are sore as boils." The Head Keeper, seeing that Charlie was wearing new boots, remarked, "You always want to wear a pair of boots a fortnight before you put them on!" It does sound a bit Irish, but there is sense in it. What the Head Keeper meant was, Charlie should have worn them for short periods to break them in, before wearing them on a hard day's pheasant shooting.

This reminds me that the 2nd Duke always had his shoes and leather gloves "broken in" for him. It was the valet's job to find someone who took the same size to do this job, but I don't think it was too popular a task as great care had to be taken with what would be the very best shoes and gloves. But that is how it was in those pre-war days.

4

Grouse shooting has always been recognised as the best of sports and the "Glorious Twelfth" looked forward to with much anticipation. Bend-Or, being very fond of all outdoor sports, of course had his grouse shooting. There is a certain amount on the vast Grosvenor Estate in Sutherlandshire, although there it is mainly fishing and stalking, but the nearest grouse shooting to Eaton is the Welsh moors. His Grace usually had the shooting of one of those, and in 1930 it was Llanarmon Dyffryn Ceiriog. I was to go with Fred Milton, the Duke's loader, so it was early September 1930 when I first saw the splendour of the grouse moor. Leaving Eaton early one morning with Fred in one of the Eaton cars, it was a pleasant run through Wrexham, Chirk and the well-wooded Welsh valleys to the Hand Hotel at Llanarmon. As usual we were in plenty of time, with His Grace and party not expected until 10 am, so it was an opportunity to chat to the moorland keepers. The moors above Llanarmon were usually pretty good, producing good bags of grouse for their size, but the Welsh keepers would rarely express optimism: just a hope that everything would go off all right and that the weather would remain good. The day itself depends so much on good weather, as a moor on a wet, windy, cold day is just about as desolate a place as you can find.

While we were waiting for the Duke, I stood by the brook that runs through the village. I saw a black and white bird skim over the water and land on a boulder quite close to me. I was fascinated by its actions, its tail bobbing up and down and head moving from side to side, like a wagtail. Shortly it jumped off the rock and proceeded to walk under the water! I was amazed at this and the Head Keeper, Jack Saint (son of Joe, the retired keeper at Eaton), must have seen me staring because he asked, "Have you never seen one before?" Well, I hadn't, and Jack told me that it was a dipper, a bird about the same size as a blackbird but with very different habits. Later I discovered that its favourite nesting place was under a small waterfall, or failing that under a bridge, but always close to water. Feeding mainly on aquatic insects and caddis, it was quite common throughout North Wales and a most attractive bird.

As the time approached ten o'clock, frequent glances were cast down the valley to look for the car carrying the Duke and his shooting party. Sure enough, in the distance could be seen the vehicles winding their way up the twisting road. There was a flurry of activity as the loaders, all local men apart from Fred, gathered the guns and other impedimenta in preparation for the walk up to the moors. Land Rovers, Sno-Cats and even tractors were not thought of in those days, and in any case I think the guests enjoyed the exercise and scenery.

After the usual "good mornings" the party moved off, and well I remember that walk. We climbed steeply over fairly rough paths and, being well laden with cartridges, coats and lunch boxes, those of us used to flat country found it rather heavy going. By now the sun was high in the sky and the temperature rising rapidly, so the shady patches were very welcome. Once on the moor itself shade was non-existent, but oh, what a marvellous sight! The purple heather in full bloom stretched as far as the eye could see, with patches of green bracken, some of it tinged with brown. The few clouds passing the sun gave the area the look of a patchwork quilt.

It was not far to the first butts, but there was not a beater in sight. Jack Saint had disappeared and I had no idea when or where he had gone. Reaching the butts, quite large hides about seventy yards apart constructed of slate or stone and well covered with turf, the five guests took up their positions. His Grace did not go to the furthermost point as was his custom when pheasant shooting, but took the first butt we came to. There was plenty of room for three so each guest, with only a loader, had even more room. Fred had instructed me on the drill and my job was to try to "mark down" any birds His Grace shot. I soon discovered that this wasn't as easy as it sounded.

After a wait of ten minutes or so several shots were fired from the further butts, but I had not set eye on a grouse. It wasn't long, though, before a single grouse came high over His Grace, and with a single shot he brought it tumbling down into the heather, well behind the butt. I tried to mark it down, making a mental note of a small rock position in relation to the dead grouse. Looking in that direction a few minutes later, I could see several small rocks poking above the heather! That didn't help me one

little bit, but no matter – soon the grouse came over, covey after covey of them, and before long a number of birds were lying in the same area as the first one. Fortunately I kept count of the number of birds down, because when the drive was over that was the first question the Duke asked!

The beaters eventually appeared in the far distance, walking through the tall heather up to forty yards apart. Each was waving a flag, which helped to put the grouse up and also helped the keeper to see their position, such a vast area of moor was being driven. As the beaters got closer, men waving flags appeared on the right and left – flank men, positioned to stop the grouse breaking out instead of going over the well-hidden butts. Jack Saint was with the man on the left, which surprised me as at a pheasant shoot the Head Keeper would more likely stay with guns. Men with dogs appeared from some distance behind, one dog man for each butt. These dog men were told the number of grouse there should be around each butt, and for some time His Grace stood outside the butt, watching the dog men pick up the grouse he had shot.

Eventually the party moved off to the next drive. The beaters had set off as soon as the first was over, and were now out of sight. It was not a long walk before we came to the next line of butts and each gun was soon in position, ready and waiting. Shortly the grouse came flashing across the moor, skimming the heather. Having plumage so much like the colourings of the moor, they were very difficult to see. Sometimes they were almost right on the butt before one spotted them. His Grace, an excellent shot, on several occasions killed a right-and-left in front and, changing guns, a right-and-left behind. Four birds out of one covey would be difficult to improve upon!

By now the sun was high in the sky and, despite the height we were at, almost too warm for comfort. When the second drive was over a halt was called for lunch and, after walking a short distance round a bend in the valley, we came upon a large wooden hut — the lunch hut. To my surprise, two men in morning suits appeared at the door as we approached — footmen from Eaton! They had come to attend to the wants of His Grace and his guests, having followed the shooting party up from Chester and climbed up to the lunch hut from a different direction from the valley below!

His Grace and his guests went inside the hut where a table and chairs could be seen and which, with the windows and door open, was no doubt a pleasantly cool spot. The keepers, beaters, loaders and dog men, finding what little shade there was, sat down on the heather by a brook which wended its way to the larger stream in the valley itself. The men who had been doing the driving were obviously glad of an opportunity to sit down and mop their brows as it is really hard work, walking for several hours in long heather over rough terrain. The lunch boxes were brought out and the contents polished off. There was much talk of the prospects for the rest of the day and Jack Saint said, "Well, lads, you'll have to work that bit harder this afternoon," at the same time pointing with his stick to a distant ridge. Of course all eyes looked that way, and there could be seen what appeared to be two huge birds swooping down low over the heather and then, with hardly a wing movement, soaring high in the sky. I thought they were eagles, but as I must have appeared mystified, Fred asked, "Do you know what they are, lad?" I had to admit that I didn't, but before Fred could answer, one of the beaters volunteered the information that they were buzzards. He went on to explain that several pairs had taken to nesting in the vicinity and, although they would kill young grouse and rabbits, their main diet consisted of beetles, worms and the like. He also explained Jack's remark about having to work harder during the afternoon. With two buzzards and probably more wheeling about the mountain tops, the grouse would sit very tight and it would need more effort from the beaters to put them over the butts.

However, the beaters did their job well and two more drives were held in the afternoon before the party made its way down into the valley from the moor. The number of brace of grouse killed? I can't remember, but the party seemed well satisfied and after His Grace had thanked everyone the shooting party got into the cars and left for Eaton. It must have been the regular routine, but as soon as the guests had departed, the doors of the Hand Hotel opened and very soon the keepers and beaters were quenching their thirsts! The landlord was no doubt pleased to have a few early customers, and certainly the men involved in the day on the moors were pleased to patronise him. Before the days of many motor cars, there would not be a lot of visitors to a pub right at the end of a valley, no matter how delightful the valley is. Even long summer days and lovely weather would entice only the dedicated hiker to journey such a distance.

After an hour or so men started to leave, many of them having to travel some distance and of course mostly on foot. The greater number of beaters were men of the hills – they had to be! – and they came from small hill-farms, so on arrival home they probably had to do almost another day's work. Fred eventually decided to leave, so we loaded up the car with a number of grouse and set off for Eaton. It was an hour's journey back to the Hall, then the guns had to be cleaned and the cartridge bags emptied and cleaned with saddle soap with just a touch of polish. The lad would clean the leatherwork, not being entrusted with the Purdeys. Cartridge bags were always emptied, because if hung full of ammunition for any length of time they tended to go out of shape. The grouse, by now cold and set, were hung in the larder, a cool and fly-proof place. Next morning two brace of grouse would be packed in ventilated cardboard boxes and placed with each guest's luggage before his departure. The birds not required at Eaton were disposed of by Jack Saint at Llanarmon, more than likely through a game dealer.

There was a lot that impressed me on that first visit to the grouse moor. It is difficult to pinpoint what I found most pleasing, but I suppose the distant views, wonderful scenery and of course the grouse themselves. The dogs, too, were remarkable, retrieving the birds out of the vast expanse of fairly dense cover. One retrieve sticks out in my memory. It was a wounded bird, just wing-tipped I should imagine, and after the dog had hunted a patch of heather for some time, it suddenly put its nose down on a sheep track and took off like the wind, disappearing over a ridge. After about five minutes it came back, tail wagging, with the grouse still alive in its mouth – a proud dog and a proud owner.

On the subject of dogs on the moor, quite a few years later Tom Lamont was working his dog (the plover-egg finder) picking up grouse. There were quite a few birds down and, after retrieving a fair number the dog picked up a bird and started towards Tom with it. Halfway to him the dog paused and put its head on one side, then up jumped a wounded grouse and went away, just managing to fly. Without more ado, Tom's dog carefully placed the bird he was carrying on top of the heather and went off like a streak after the wounded bird. Soon he caught it and returned to

his master with the bird, which was still alive. As soon as Tom had taken the bird off the dog, it spun round and returned for the bird it had carefully placed on top of the heather. Do dogs have intelligence or was this instinct? I am not going to argue that one!

Several days each year were spent on the moors at Llanarmon but very large bags were rare. His Grace was very fond of his Scottish estate and the grouse shooting at Llanarmon must have given him the flavour of Scotland without the long journey from Eaton! Incidentally, His Grace as far as I am aware never went to shoot on another estate, not even for pheasant, though he did once go shooting in Albania with the King of that country. Snipe were plentiful but bags were not large; they were driven birds and the native beaters were rather voluble, sending the birds in all directions but not over the guns. I had all this from Fred Milton, who went on the trip as a passenger on the yacht *Cutty Sark* – for him it was the most enjoyable shooting trip ever.

One gentleman at Llanarmon the first time I was there, Brigadier Sir Joseph Laycock, was the complete opposite to His Grace as far as his shooting was concerned. Some time during the 'thirties his valet told me that the Brigadier was booked up for shooting from the "Glorious Twelfth" right through the shooting season until the early spring, when wildfowling on tidal waters brought shooting to a close. No-one envied the valet having to do all that travelling, frequently driving the Brigadier's Rolls half the night whilst the owner dozed in the back seat – a very trying winter, one would imagine! Brigadier Sir Joseph Laycock was the father of General Sir Robert Laycock, who led the raid on Rommel's headquarters in the Middle East during the Second World War. Unfortunately Rommel wasn't at home!

During this same month of September 1930 several days partridge shooting took place at Eaton. The "little brown birds" were reared on the Aldford beat, which at that time was a more suitable environment, although it was not good enough for the partridge to do very well in the wild state. George Grass was in charge of the rearing and by September had them distributed over the Aldford beat where they could be shown to the best advantage. Five or six guns were usually the maximum out partridge shooting and although quite large areas were driven, a comparatively small number of beaters were used. Driving partridge is very like driving grouse and in fact the shooting is very similar, but the surroundings were not quite as attractive as the moorland. The beaters wore their familiar red hats and white smocks which, since they were out on open farmland as opposed to thick woodland, made a wonderful spectacle. Usually four drives, two before and two after lunch, were the order of the day. Dick Starks was always present but usually stood at the end of the line of guns and observed all that went on, after giving a blast on his whistle for the drive to start.

His Grace was an excellent shot at partridge and very few that were within range got past him, unless they came in large coveys which hand-reared birds tend to do. Fred did not need a lad to carry the cartridge bag for him when partridge shooting, so I took a place with the line of beaters, keeping close to one of the keepers, Jim Saint, whose brother was Jack Saint at Llanarmon. The first day I was with the beaters was an education; previously I had been with the line of guns and only seen what I suppose you might call the end product. Beating is not as easy as is generally supposed. It is not just a question of walking, in this case across a field, but the beaters must keep in a straight line, possibly with several men on the flanks to turn the birds over the guns. George Grass was in charge of the beaters and was an expert at driving partridge. The beaters did not need much instruction but had to keep their eye on "the General", as George was called. He always indicated by hand signals what he wanted, and anyone who ignored his signal was told in no uncertain terms about it at the end of the drive. All the beaters were Estate workers so knew exactly what was required of them. It was usually the lads that had to be drawn to order, but I was fortunate to be tagging on to Jim Saint so there were no problems as far as I was concerned.

Only a comparatively small number of partridges were reared, but it was surprising how much good sport they could provide. By taking the first three drives towards one particular area, it was possible to have the bulk of the birds in the last drive of the day by beating that area. This made a marvellous finish to the day, but to ensure that the coveys did not return to their home ground, "stops" (beaters left in strategic positions) had to be put out while lunch was being taken. His Grace and party always returned to the Hall for lunch and sometimes this would entail a two-hour break, which meant that stops had to be particularly vigilant to prevent the movement of the coveys. The land had a good deal of ground cover, and this made it possible for the little brown bird to run from one drive to another unobserved.

One season the last drive on the first shoot did not turn out as had been expected. A large number of birds had been put into the area for the afternoon's sport, but the first drive after lunch was only reasonable, and of course it was hoped that most of the birds had gone further on and would be put over the guns in a grand slam to finish the day. But barely as many were brought back over the waiting guns as had escaped in the previous drive. Dick Starks swore blind that the stops had not done their job properly during the lunch break but His Grace, although obviously disappointed, said, "Never mind, Starks, we'll catch up with them next week."

The following week duly arrived and after the morning drives had been made, the stops sent out and the shooting party taken off for lunch, Dick produced a sack containing some long object and sent for his son, Togo. "A job 'ere for 'ee, lad," he said, and took from the bag a kite! "I'll stop them little devils getting half a mile away from us, like last time." He told Togo to go to a large field half a mile away and to fly the kite as high as possible, making it rise and fall just beyond the last drive. Dick then opened up the kite for everyone to see, and it was cut out in the shape of a huge hawk! Togo set off, taking one of the lads with him, and of course

all eyes were eventually looking in the direction the kite should have been flying. It did just appear at a very low height once or twice, but what Dick had overlooked was the fact that there was practically no wind, so Togo was on a loser even before he started. That day the last drive was a great success, but no-one ever knew whether it was the hawk kite or Togo cursing that kept the partridges in the drive.

Partridges were still reared after the Second World War, but after the passing of Bend-Or not quite so many of them. The 4th Duke, the well-beloved "Gerald Duke" as he was universally known, was keen on partridge shooting, but as the years passed and such vast changes took place in farming it became a useless exercise. During the 'thirties large fields had been divided into "town pieces". These were acres or half-acres, each usually having a different crop on it and being rented by villagers who kept cattle. Sometimes you would see eight or nine different crops on one of these town pieces — ideal for partridge. Of course there were no tractors as all work on the land was done by horse-drawn machinery and sometimes by hand, even in the early 1930s. I can remember one villager digging half an acre in the town piece and growing massive vegetable marrows — I never did know what he did with them but surely he wouldn't eat all that much chutney! Of course the small areas of corn, mainly oats and wheat, were cut by the old-fashioned reaper and tied by hand, although later the binder appeared which speeded things up a bit. So with horse-drawn machinery, patches of various types of crops and dogs not allowed under any circumstances, there was generally reasonable peace for the hand-reared birds.

During the last twenty years there have been such radical changes in farming methods that our indigenous game bird of the lowlands has little encouragement in vast areas of the country. At Eaton as elsewhere, farms have tended to become larger and larger, tractors and implements larger and larger and, I suppose worst of all, hedges pulled up to make fields larger and larger. It must end some time, but even pheasants are suffering from this intensive method of farming. They say it is all in the cause of economy. Maybe, but I ask myself the question, "What of the future?" I have noticed over the last ten years or so that the amount of fertiliser used has increased dramatically. The use of sprays of various sorts is so commonplace that hardly a field escapes and as far as I can see the good old farmyard muck has almost gone, its place taken by slurry. This is a noxious liquid which if spread on the land too thickly can even kill the herbage. Oh dear, have the modern methods been an improvement?

One thing is certain: the new farming has reduced the number of people living and working in the country and to me this is a bad thing. Some of the old country skills have gone for ever. For example, woodmen today use a power saw when felling timber. It is a noisy tool and part of the rural scene now, needing a certain amount of skill but nothing compared to that of the old-time woodmen. Putting a face on a tree, so that it fell in the right direction, was always done with an axe, and to see a skilled man swinging an axe and the chips flying created a wonderful picture. Similarly, the mechanical hedge-cutter makes a neat, tidy job but is very noisy, and it does not remove the elders and briars out of the hedges like the farm-hand with the brushing hook would.

Another advantage of the old days, when a large number of men were working on the land, was the information passed on to the keepers by them. They would tell you if vermin were about, the position of partridge and pheasant nests, and of course of any signs of poaching activities. Some of them would never mention if a stoat was about for the simple reason that stoats killed a lot of rabbits. The farm-hand would be only too eager to get a rabbit for the table and the ones killed by stoats were always the best around. Keepers used to overcome this problem by being generous with rabbits and always maintaining a friendly relationship.

Coming back to the hedge cutting, it was the practice on the Home Farm, where most of the partridge shooting took place, for the hedge-cutting gang to leave the hedge for a distance of about five yards in certain positions. These patches of up to six feet made quite good butts or hides for the guns to stand behind, and of course were a permanent feature. Today the hedging machine takes everything in front of it, though I have noticed on several farms that some strong saplings are being left in the hopes that in the future we shall see trees in the hedgerows.

So many changes have taken place over the last two decades, and many things common in the past have disappeared. The cowslip is seldom seen today, that lovely plant with its yellow flowers giving such a nice touch of colour to the banks and ditches. Sprays must be responsible for its disappearance, as they are for so many more of the once common wild flowers. Even the wild sage, which Ted Milton used to add to the pheasant chicks' feed, is certainly not to be found where it used to be.

The bird population has changed so much too. It is no longer possible during the spring months to hear the corncrake, at one time a regular nesting bird in Cheshire. Its rasping call morning and evening was a joy to listen to. Its cousin, the water rail, a very shy and retiring bird, was also plentiful; now, alas, it is very rarely seen or even heard in the spring in this area. When plover-egging in the 'thirties it was not unusual to find a redshank's nest; no longer does it nest on the water meadows at Eaton. The chiff-chaff still heralds the coming of spring but in smaller numbers, and many of the warblers are not as plentiful. The grasshopper warbler used to nest in quite large numbers, but in 1979 two pairs were all I could account for.

Eaton, like all other estates, has to run on a sound financial basis and in many respects is much better than most. The present Duke (the 6th) is very keen on the preservation of the environment, but of course his good intentions are limited by the needs of modern farming. Nevertheless many steps have been taken, such as the re-planting of small areas of what would be waste ground. For example, corners of fields where the huge modern farm machinery cannot operate have, on His Grace's instructions, been planted with usually a hardwood – ash, oak or beech. Often the corner has been fenced off, creating quite a nice area for small birds and game alike. The large areas of softwoods so often planted by the Forestry Commission are probably the most viable crop but do not provide much of a suitable habitat for the vast majority of wildlife: they create a dense canopy and after the first few years smother all the ground cover. Nor are they a very suitable environment for most of our birdlife, although owls seem to like these dense woodlands, where they eat a vast number of beetles. The tawny owl in particular is quite happy in such surroundings, and all the softwoods I know have their quota of tawny owls. It is often possible to hear them hooting during the daytime, when they will sit out in the sun. Small birds normally mob any predator, but in this type of wood the owls will hoot gaily away without being buzzed by the normal host of chaffinches and others – a sure sign that these dark woodlands are not popular with our smaller bird population.

In the old days of coal fires at the Hall, the woodmen had the annual task of cutting "faggots". These were bundles of brushwood about a yard long, tied with a band made from red withies. The faggots usually consisted of young sycamore saplings and several woods on the estate were reserved to provide this essential fire-lighting material. An area was cleared each winter and it was about six years before this same piece could provide another crop. When enough faggots had been cut they were carted to Eaton by the waggoners and stacked under a building like the modern hay bay. There was always twelve months supply of faggots on hand so that they were seasoned and dry and able to be lit easily. Coal was carried to Eaton on the narrow-gauge railway, travelling a distance of about three miles through the Estate from the railway yard at Balderton. Today, no faggots, no railway, hardly any woodmen! Electricity provides the cooking power, oil fuel the heating in the new modern Hall.

On the Estate as a whole, so many things have changed. The villages are no longer full of young people, all looking forward to a job on Eaton Estate. Most school leavers go into the city to work; even if there is a job available in the rural area they seem to prefer the city lights. Part of this may be due to the education today. All village children on reaching eleven years old have to go to school in urban areas and it seems to me they are becoming urbanised. Also, a lot of people coming to live in the country come from built up areas and often do not appreciate the delights of the countryside at all seasons. They even press the Parish Council for street lighting. Street lighting! Why put up such unsightly things in delightful villages when most people today, if only going two hundred yards, go in the car? Unfortunately the older people will soon be gone and no doubt the face of many villages will change. At the moment the policy on Eaton Estate is not to build in the villages, thus retaining their rural character, but with such a big demand for building land, how long can it last?

Practically all the people living in the rural villages before the war were real countrymen and good naturalists, many of them without knowing it. They could forecast the weather quite accurately, sometimes by just listening to the birds. The great tit, or "saw-whet" as the old hands called it, always indicated rain when making a certain call, and that of course is just as true today. The appearance of certain wading birds on the meadow also indicated bad weather to come, and at a certain time of the autumn they were a sure sign that it would be a hard winter, with lots of snow. I suppose that people today turn the radio or television on and get the forecast from that, but what fun to observe all that goes on in nature and try to work out your own weather forecast from what you see and hear.

Yes, the scene has changed, and there is one incident of which I have never really worked out the logic. Several years ago the new occupant of a cottage in the village complained to me that her cat was missing. I politely told her that I had not seen it, in fact didn't even know what it was like. Several days later the same lady met me in the lane and accused me of killing her "Tommy". I hadn't, and told her so. She was a newcomer to life in the country, and obviously thought the keeper must be responsible for Tommy's absence. Cats sometimes have to be dealt with but country people realise this and if they have a cat that kills game they expect it to meet an early end. In fact, on other occasions I have been asked to put a cat down when the owner realised the damage it was capable of. Although this poor soul was obviously very fond of her cat, I couldn't help her except by saying, "He'll come back in a day or so." I hoped, since she called it Tommy, that it was a tom cat as they are very apt to stray. But she would not be pacified and threatened to report me to the R.S.P.C.A. and the police. I suggested she did just that, but her remark as she left puzzled me greatly; it was "and I'll never give another penny to the Church in my life." I still haven't found out the reasoning behind that remark, as I am not connected in any official way with the Parish Church! The only thing that annoyed me about the incident was that when I saw her with a cat in her arms a week or so later, I enquired if Tommy had returned – all I got was a black look and her back turned to me. I was told by a neighbour that Tommy had indeed returned so the least the lady could have done was to have told me so. I just hope the Church didn't lose out.

5

In 1931 the 2nd Duke decided to rent another shoot and give some of the woods at Eaton a rest for a year or two to reduce the ever-present risk of disease among such a density of pheasants as the Eaton woods had. Major Kerr was fortunate to be able to lease a shoot at Llangollen, some twenty miles away, called "Worlds End". It is an attractive valley running west of Llangollen, and up to the Ruabon Moors. About four miles up the valley the steep hillsides are well wooded with smaller valleys to the left, also with woods on either side. This made it an ideal situation for the type of pheasant shooting His Grace loved – good high birds with every one a sporting shot. In fact some of them turned out to be out of range!

Tom Lamont was to move into a small farmhouse halfway up the valley, central for the control of the shoot, and took up residence there soon after the shooting season ended at Eaton. A bungalow was being built in a very pleasant spot to accommodate the keepers who would each be in charge of a beat. Seven keepers would be moving in when the bungalow was completed, some from Eaton and several new ones. I was included in the Eaton staff moving up into the hills, which I suppose was really an honour, taking over a beat in untried country after only two years' experience. With Tom Lamont in charge to ensure that things were as His Grace wanted them, I was looking forward to the move, but most of the birds were going to be reared at Eaton so I expected to go to Worlds End with the poults in July. However, some staff were needed to go there as soon as the bungalow was completed and new men were moving in. It was late April when the move came and the valleys and hills were clad in numerous shades of green, with some patches of russet where the previous year's bracken still stood. Lambs were gambolling in the fields and everywhere looked fresh and bright in the spring sunshine. I was with one of the keepers from Eaton, Frank Milton, Fred's brother, who had just returned from looking after the pack of boar-hounds on the Duke's French estate. We were to share a room in the now completed bungalow. A cook was to be engaged to look after the wants of the seven keepers and would arrive within a week, but Frank and myself were the only occupants for a day or so. Tom Lamont's wife was very kind and had got some food in for us, and better still invited both of us to a hot meal at eventide.

After several days the cook arrived and we soon settled down to a routine. Our task was to get the woods ready to receive the poults when they came up from Eaton. The woods at Worlds End were not wired round with fox-proof wire netting, as this would have been an almost impossible job on the stony, steep hillsides. It meant that the pheasants would be able to stray much more freely and earlier than at Eaton, but the nature of the valley ensured that the birds would still be in another wood. However, woodmen were already fencing the perimeter of the woods to ensure that the sheep did not stray in: most woods were open to the moors, so sheep would seek shelter when the weather was bad. Those woodmen were highly skilled, and apart from the sheep-netting almost all the stakes and posts were made on site. Oak was used, medium-sized trees being felled, cut into appropriate lengths with cross-cut saws, then split by axe and wedge to the size required. These stakes and posts are much more durable than similar things cut on a saw-bench as the rain runs down the outside of the grain when it is split, whereas it enters sawn wood and shortens its life. I would not be a bit surprised if the perimeter fence is still standing, at least in parts.

However, our job was not concerned with that aspect of the shoot but more with taking steps to ensure that the minimum number of poults was going to be lost to vermin. Tunnel traps were essential, as the large numbers of rabbits suggested that there was also likely to be a good stoat population. Each wood that was going to have pheasants released in it needed a fair number of traps, but fortunately plenty of slate and small rocks were at hand to build a tunnel wherever needed. It was very largely trial and error where the traps were positioned, but any walls or brooks close to the woods usually proved satisfactory, and in several places clefts in large boulders also turned out to be effective. Once all the traps were placed they had to be visited every day and any captives removed, while we sometimes found it necessary to re-site a trap after it had been in one position for a time and not made a catch. Whilst busy with the trap-setting we kept our eyes open for carrion crows and magpie nests. There were not many of the latter but far too many of the "large black 'uns".

Unfortunately it was rather late in the spring to deal with the crows on the nest. The normal practice in those days was to sneak up to the nest and shoot the hen-bird as it left, but by this time all the crows had hatched their eggs and were busy feeding their young. It looks as if crows can only count up to one because an effective trick was for two men to walk up to the nest, one of them taking up a concealed position within range of the crow returning to the nest, and the second man walking away as conspicuously as possible. It usually took twenty minutes for the crow to come to the nest and, with a bit of luck, it would fall to the gun of the waiting keeper. Frank Milton was a crack shot, so I usually walked away and left the most important part to him. Once a crow was accounted for a shot would be fired into the nest to destroy the young birds. This left a large number of single birds, and although in my opinion crows and many other birds pair for life, on losing a mate they will frequently re-pair. These single birds had to be dealt with, so gin traps were set in the area known to be frequented by them. Being legal in those days, traps were set in the open, half-fenced with twigs. The bait was a piece of rabbit or a couple of eggs at the back, and with luck the crow would step on the lightly set trap at the entrance. Many crows were accounted for by these methods, and of course the traps picked up other predators such as magpies, stoats and weasels.

Foxes were found to be plentiful and had to be dealt with. No hunting took place in this Welsh valley so it was in order to kill as many as possible. Many of these foxes came down off the moors. The hill-farmers hated them, and we moor keepers were anxious to deal with as many as possible. They would bring their cubs down off the tops in September and, if not dealt with quickly, make a fine mess amongst the growing poults. In those days, trapping was the main method of dealing with Reynard. Extra-large traps were used and were normally set in any large hole the fox was likely to use. We found that by keeping a number of these traps set we could pick up many foxes before they really took up residence in the area. Terriers were sometimes used, but their role was restricted to pushing the fox out for the waiting keepers to shoot as in that rocky terrain most earths were impossible to dig.

Buzzards were fairly common and many were dealt with, some by baited traps and others by shooting. I am now convinced that the number of game birds buzzards kill is small, as they feed mainly on lesser mammals and numerous beetles. I have watched through glasses a buzzard turn over a dead rabbit and take what was underneath, then fly off without touching the flesh of the rabbit. Any carcass lying around for a day or two attracts beetles and other insects, and I am sure that was what the buzzard was after. At the same time, I have known the big, brown, handsome bird to take ten-week-old pheasants so they are not completely blameless. Perhaps the greatest damage they do to a wood full of pheasants is to disturb them. A buzzard's appearance high in the sky over a track full of feeding pheasants causes pandemonium; the birds just explode, disappearing in all directions, and are a long time before coming back to feed, no matter how hungry they are. One can imagine the chaos caused if buzzards spend a lot of time in or over one wood, whose occupants will eventually depart for a more peaceful abode. Even mature pheasants will seek cover when a buzzard appears, but I am certain it is the size of the bird rather than the possibility of attack that really scares the living daylights out of pheasants in particular.

As the summer progressed we caught one or two polecats in the tunnel traps, and also one pine marten. I was sorry about that, the marten being a fairly rare animal, and althought it might have taken a few pheasants, I think we could have suffered that in the cause of preservation. Pine martens have been seen in the Welsh mountains not all that far from Rhyl in the last fifteen years, so maybe there are still a few left. Many years later, at Eaton, polecats killed many poults in one wood and, though eventually dealt with, do re-appear periodically. They are not easy to catch, being mostly nocturnal, and as they spend a lot of their time in the trees they can take pheasants up to a good age off the roost. They rarely return to a half-eaten victim which makes the chances of getting the culprit pretty remote, but a well-sited tunnel trap can prove effective.

After three months' concentrated attack on the resident predators by Frank, the two other keepers, Duncan Stewart and Ken Inman, and myself, the time approached for the young pheasants to come up from the Eaton rearing fields. The woodmen had cleared feeding tracks in the woods and coops started to arrive to put the broody hens and poults in. They were unloaded as close as possible to the tracks, but the woods being on steep hillsides meant that it was a manual job to get the coops into place. Four of us took several hours to carry one load of coops to the required position, but eventually several woods were ready to receive their birds.

The day arrived for the first lot of poults to be delivered from Eaton. They were to go to the top of the valley in a wood called the "Black Wood", so called because of numerous clumps of Norway spruce in it. All was ready to receive them: coops in position, water in motor tyres cut in half round the circumference and food ready cooked in the boiler. About 8 am, the lorry carrying the moving boxes could be seen winding its way up the lane. When it had arrived at the nearest point to the wood, the boxes were transferred to a horse and cart which was able to move along the coops and unload its precious cargo. The broody hen and poults were put in the coops, one box-load to a coop, and, following the same routine as at Eaton, kept in for several hours before the birds were let out and fed. About one hundred and twenty coops were to be the allocation per wood, which with seven keepers and seven woods amounted to a lot of pheasants. A full load of boxes on the lorry was eighty, each box with an average of fifteen poults, so even at twelve hundred birds a load, a good many journeys would be made before all the woods were filled. After the first load of boxes things began to build up and two or three loads would arrive each week, but many of the woods could not be reached by lorry or cart, so it meant manpower. The woodmen and keepers were all involved in this and, with each man having hold of one end of a box and climbing one behind the other up the steep hillside, must have looked from the distance like giant ants on an ant hill!

Frank Milton was to be in charge of the Black Wood, and so that he was able to see how I went on, the birds in the adjoining wood were put in my care. Like his brother, Fred, he was always good company and taught me a lot of keepering. We shared the same food hut, where instead of the usual single boiler two were available for cooking the food. After the pheasants were let out of the coops it was a question of feeding them three times a day, at the same time every day, and not giving them too much to eat. A hungry bird answers the call much better at feed time, so it was most important that all the food was eaten at every feed.

Disturbance is another great factor, which causes the loss of countless pheasant poults every year; if disturbed soon after being released, the young birds get lost and usually die from malnutrition, because they are not used at that age to fending for themselves. This disturbance causes as much havoc today when birds are released in large numbers from the brooder houses, possibly more so as there is no broody hen to call them back.

As the summer progressed we were to get a lot of disturbance from the human element. For many years the valley had been a favourite haunt of hikers taking the pleasant walk either up the valley and over the moor to the outskirts of Wrexham, or along the high ridge from Crow Castle to Minera, again not far from Wrexham. The farmers in the valley had not been too perturbed about this trespass, so long as gates were closed and no fires lighted. We could not look on these pleasure-seeking visitors with quite so much benevolence, and many times had to re-direct people from the pheasant woods. I remember one very hot afternoon when, after hearing voices in a wood, I discovered a number of young men and women sitting on the coops in bathing costumes, having their photographs taken. Bikinis weren't heard of then, but the bright colours of the costumes were enough to make those particular pheasants very shy at coming to feed for several days!

Tom Lamont was dead nuts on trespassers that were disturbing game and, being a Scotsman, was very fond of using a telescope. He would spend hours on top of the Maiden Rock, which was the highest point, observing the movements right down the valley below. From that vantage point on a bright sunny day, and it was usually good weather when the visitors came, he would signal with a mirror when someone appeared to be transgressing. He expected all the keepers to be extra-vigilant when they saw his signal from that three-hundred-foot rock, and it proved most helpful on many occasions. It was surprising how far down the valley the flashing mirror could be seen.

One evening I was walking back from the Maiden Rock with Tom when we spotted something white in the distance. As we got nearer, it became obvious it was someone erecting a tent about two hundred yards from the public road, beside a brook which tumbled down through a very nice wood, the "Oak Wood". Tom was furious and his face, always well-coloured, became as red as the

now setting sun. We left the road and approached the man and woman who had just about got the tent into position; in fact the man was picking up a few twigs, with the obvious intention of lighting a fire. That didn't help Tom's temper! Trying to control it, he asked them politely to remove the tent and get back to the public road. Understandably, the man was not a bit amused and flatly refused to do so. This made matters worse. Tom, a man who would brook no argument, growled, "You'll be moving it within five minutes." Again the man refused, saying that he was doing no harm and had no intention of moving.

Tom could stand no more. He kicked a cooking pan into the brook and started to pull up the guy ropes of the tent. The man rushed at him, but stopped short when Tom lifted his stick. I must admit Tom did look rather a fearsome sight, with his rather tubby figure garbed in plus fours and a deerstalker hat, his red glowing face, and brandishing a stick. The man, standing open-mouthed, knew not what to do, but was soon left in no doubt when Tom roared at him, "You'll be a-moving this tent, or I'll throw you and it in the burn!" I've never seen a tent come down so quickly, and soon they were on the road heading back for Llangollen. The woman had stood and watched speechless, and I'm not surprised. Things like that happened in the 'thirties but I wonder what would be the outcome of a similar incident today. Fortunately cars were few and far between. I haven't been up to Worlds End for many years, but I don't doubt that it is alive with motor traffic during the good weather.

The pheasants were doing well on this fresh ground with its abundance of insects and herbage and, although there was no wire around the woods to restrain them, did not stray as much as we really expected them to. There had to be constant vigilance for predators and for any disturbance. Night time was the greatest risk for young birds usually "jug" on the ground before going to roost at eight or nine weeks old. It only needed a fox to get amongst the poults and the losses would be heavy, so a night time vigil was kept. This entailed two keepers being on duty throughout the night, their job to patrol from wood to wood and keep fires going on rocky outcrops – the mountain and moorland foxes were not so domesticated as those on the lower ground and it took much less to scare them of. Alarm guns were used as well; these worked by clockwork and could be set to fire a blank cartridge at given intervals. The night duty keeper had to attend to them, starting them off at dusk and sometimes re-loading them through the night. Although the night work came to an end after several weeks, once the poults had taken to going to roost, the alarm guns were still set but to go off at longer intervals throughout the night. This night work had to be done, but at least the short summer darkness soon passed.

The sounds of a summer night are very different from those of the long winter darkness. Soon after dusk, the hedgehogs start to feed, making a snorting sound as they root amongst the pine needles for beetles. An occasional shriek from an owl can be heard, often followed by the "mewing" of the young of that season, either calling for food or keeping in touch with the parent birds. It was a wonderful sight to see the rays of the sun appear over the mountains and the valley start to come to life. The birds gave quite a welcome to the new day, although high summer was too late in the year for the real "dawn chorus". The rabbits scuttled to the safety of their burrows after feeding in the dark, and what I remember most is the din made by the jackdaws which nested on the face of the cliffs, as they mobbed the peregrine falcon when it appeared from its eyrie.

Frank Milton was a great help to me in this my first season looking after pheasants, and we spent many happy hours while he told me of his past experiences. Our cabin was some distance from the bungalow where we lived, so to give ourselves as much time with the pheasants as possible, we used to take lunch and tea with us. We could brew tea on a primus stove in the cabin and do a limited amount of cooking. Manor House Farm was reasonably close and we were able to get fresh milk from Mr Worthington, the farmer. He also let us help ourselves to his gooseberries and raspberries. We had many a marvellous meal, and I don't know of anything better than cooking freshly gathered food in the open, in the countryside. Frank was very fond of fish, and the small streams which came tumbling down the valleys held numerous trout, not very large, maybe nine to ten inches long. I had seen these often, but as I stood and watched they seemed to vanish. Frank knew how

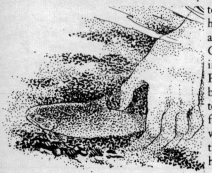

to catch them, though. One day he said, "Get some fat in that pan and warm it up. I won't be long." Of course I did, not even thinking about fish, yet alone trout. Frank disappeared round some boulders, but after no more than ten minutes re-appeared carrying four lovely trout and said, "These will just about fill the pan" – and they did! He then told me how he had got them by "tickling".

This is an old country trick practised by poachers for centuries, but it provided us with many feeds. This particular day, I remember, the trout were followed by raspberries and cream off the top of the milk, and never was a meal more enjoyed. I didn't even mind the washing up in the brook afterwards!

They were long days, but it was a lovely summer with hardly any rain through July, August and September. Despite the drought the streams still flowed and the water cascading over rocks and ledges caused miniature waterfalls and a lovely tinkling sound. Right at the base of the Maiden Rock a spring bubbled to the surface and the ice-cold water was marvellous to drink on a blazing hot day.

It was interesting to watch the dippers walking under water in search of food, and amazing to see them training the young birds. The young would stand on a stone in the brook while the adult birds brought them feed from the shallow, clear water. Presenting the young with a beak full of feed, the adult would walk into the water before the youngsters could catch it. It wasn't long before the young plucked up courage and followed their parents into the fast-flowing water. This to me was one of the wonders of nature, but fifty years in the countryside has taught me that all nature is wonderful, and this is just one small part of it.

Kingfishers could be seen too, but only in small numbers. I suppose several pairs did breed in the area, but they are basically shy birds. Flashing low over the water beneath the overhanging boughs, presenting only a fleeting view to the casual observer, they were still something exceptional to behold. The brilliant colours of

the bird passing through a ray of sunlight captured the eye, and the odd time a kingfisher settled, usually on a dead bough, gave one the chance to admire the exquisite markings of the bird. May they always adorn our brooks and streams.

Yellow wagtails were fairly common and a much more interesting bird than the pied wagtail of lower terrain. Frequenting the same areas as the dipper and kingfisher, they also added colour to a delightful settting. Continually bobbing up and down like the pied wagtail, but with more attractive colouring, they could not fail to catch the eye. Come to think of it, the dipper bobs up and down as well. Is there a link between this action and water? I wonder.

World's End also had its fair share of visiting herons, all intent on feeding on the trout in the shallow water. In those days herons were not protected by law, in fact the fishery boards put a bounty of five shillings on a head. Any bird that appeared was hounded by bounty hunters, but I supose five shillings was a lot in the early 1930s: working it out on the basis of adult wages being about two pounds a week, that five bob was the equivalent of ten pounds today. What a good job the heron is now a protected bird. Several were shot by our keepers, including one by a fellow keeper, George Eaton. He decided to eat part of it, having read or heard that the breasts of the bird were delicious if fried. George did not pluck the bird but skinned the breast and cut the flesh away, making two nice steaks. When he had cooked these pieces in some good old-fashioned lard, he sat down to enjoy what he hoped would be a good meal. I saw him pull a wry face and asked what he thought of heron steak. He did not reply but offered me a forkful. I soon knew why the wry face! Probably the best way to describe the taste is to imagine what a nice piece of frying steak would taste like if cooked with kippers in the same pan. Not for me, nor George, and if memory serves me right the dogs weren't too keen either!

George Eaton was a Lincolnshire man of about forty, a dour, straightforward man but of a kindly nature. As we were some distance from Llangollen and worked the hours we did, it was not easy to get a haircut. George was quite good at haircutting and, although he had only the rudimentary tools, managed to make quite a respectable job of it. As it was usually dusk when the keepers returned to the bungalow, with only paraffin lamps for illumination, a good haircut was hard to come by. So it was the custom when a trim was needed to arrange with George to meet him at his cabin at "Craig Arthur". One of the keepers, Jack Parsons, whose hair had got rather long by the standard of those days, was having George give him the treatment on one occasion. Soon after starting,

Jack must have said something to which George took exception. George went quiet but pressed on with the scissor work. After cutting half of Jack's head of hair he stopped, wiped the scissors and replaced them in his holder. Jack asked if he had finished. George replied, "I've finished as far as you are concerned" and refused to cut another hair! Now Jack did look a sight but back at the bungalow that evening nothing would persuade George to finish the job off. Jack was like that for several days, until in fact George Astbury brought Dickie Starks up from Eaton. Dickie laughed until his sides ached but in the end sent George Astbury with Jack down to Llangollen to get the job finished. I would have liked to see the barber's face when Jack walked in!

Not only did such incidents as this bring a little light relief to the ever-present task of looking after the game, but about the middle of August Tom Lamont took me with him to some sheep-dog trials at Vivod on Captain Dewhurst's estate, about five miles away on the Corwen road. It was quite a long walk across country, but on a balmy August day a most enjoyable one. We arrived before lunch to find a keeper on gate duty who was known to Tom, and whom I was later to know well. Alf Matthews had been at Eaton as a lad, but now was in charge of the shooting at Vivod. He died only in 1979 after being for many years Head Keeper to Mr Jimmy McAlpine at the Llanarmon pheasant shoot, lower down the valley than the grouse shoot. Alf was keen to know how the birds were doing, and the dates of shoots were exchanged so that Alf could come to Worlds End when we were shooting and Tom could go to Vivod on their big days.

There was a huge crowd around the area where the trials were taking place and after a while I could tell that many of them must have travelled a long way. I heard a Scottish accent on several occasions, and some seemed to talk with a southern dialect. I didn't really understand what the dogs were trying to do or the way they were judged, but Tom did his best to explain it all to me. It was indeed a spectacle worth watching – the way the dogs sometimes singly, sometimes in pairs, brought the sheep from way up on the mountain, going out of sight for minutes at a time. The cutting out of three or five sheep from quite a large flock was indeed a work of art. I met Tom Jones, the shepherd from the Home Farm at Eaton, although he was not taking part, and of course Tom Lamont met several people he knew. It was a most enjoyable day, and the winners would go on to the Welsh Championship trials to be held later, elsewhere in Wales. We stopped for a drink at the Chain Bridge Hotel on our way back to Worlds End and arrived at the bungalow as dusk was falling. Tom bade me good-night, saying, "The cook should have a good feed ready now, so you'll be all right, lad."

That particular feed was all right, and the cook, also called Tom Jones, was one of the best pastry-makers I have ever known, so there was always a fruit or jam tart in the pantry. On some aspects of the culinary art, though, I'm afraid Tom Jones was sadly lacking! On one occasion that September, we decided to have one or two of the broody hens out of the coops as a meal. These hens were now about to lay and in tip-top condition, fat as butter, so if cooked correctly excellent eating. Several of these birds were brought in, having been rough-plucked in the woods, and handed to Tom Jones, who said he knew exactly what to do with them. The next evening seven keepers arrived back at the bungalow, hungry as hunters and looking forward to the chicken meal. We all sat down at the table and Tom appeared with the birds on a large platter. George Eaton always did the carving and, with a flourish of the blade on the steel, proceeded to cut slices off a bird. Shortly there was a loud hiss, and maize rattled onto the platter! George stared at this apparition, unable to believe his eyes. Nor could we. He shouted for poor old Tom to find out why the crop of the bird had not been cleaned out. It transpired that the bird had been cooked after removing the head and legs but not the insides or crop. You can imagine the look on the faces of the hungry keepers! Being as hungry as we were, we carefully carved the breasts of the bird and salvaged enough from the catastrophe to satisfy our appetites. Although the thought made it rather hard to swallow, it actually tasted good – hungry men aren't too particular when there is nothing else.

September passed and soon the shooting season was almost upon us again. There was very little driving in to be done at Worlds End since the pheasants rarely went out into the heather, which came down to the woods in most places. They were coming to feed well and were more or less safe from most predators, so the hardest part was carrying the feed to the now fully grown, hungry birds. It was essential to get the birds feeding high up in the woods to provide good sporting birds on shooting days, and I had to get a large number to feed on top of the Maiden Rock itself. This entailed a long detour to get to the top of its steep face. Carrying half a hundredweight of corn over very rough terrain was hard work, but fortunately had to be done only once a day. The night feed was lower down in the trees where the birds roosted, which was much easier to deal with.

Mid-November arrived and it was time to put the pegs out for the stands. Tom Lamont went round with each keeper and the pegs were put up in what were considered the most suitable spots for good sport, but the final decision was left to Dick Starks, who came up for the day and went round each stand. Although Tom was in control on the spot, Dick had overall responsibility and of course was anxious that all should go well. During this visit the way of driving the woods was discussed and a plan formed for handling the beaters. A number of the Eaton beaters were coming up and would be in their usual beaters' dress, but most of the beating would be done by local men familiar with the area — woodmen, shepherds and farmers. Dick decided that the Eaton men should be spaced out amongst the local men when driving a wood, thus presenting the usual colourful view to the guns.

The day came and all the usual drills were carried out so that on the arrival of His Grace and guests there was no waiting before the shooting started. The first rise was a great success, the birds crossing the valley at a good height and testing the skill of the guns below. The day progressed along the usual lines, and in the steep wooded valleys almost every bird that went over the guns was a good sporting shot. The highest birds were at the Maiden Rock rise, where one of the guests was heard to remark, "They are like a lot of b——— starlings." No doubt that was how they did appear to the guns. The rock was three hundred feet high, and the birds just flipped across a narrow valley to their roosting place on the other side. The normal effective range of a twelve-bore shotgun is forty to fifty yards, so birds coming over at nearly one hundred yards range must have been impossible targets. All the same, the bag at the end of the day was over eighteen hundred and His Grace was delighted. The next day followed the same pattern, with just about the same number accounted for after the day's shooting.

There was the usual house party at Eaton but I cannot recall the ladies coming out after lunch; maybe the journey was a bit too much for them. Lunch for the guns had been brought up from the

Hall by the household staff, as had victuals for the keepers, loaders, dog men and beaters. This was in itself a mammoth task, with some 180 men to feed. At night, as after every two-day shoot, there would be a glittering ball at Eaton. The ballroom would hold about a hundred and fifty and a London band – Sydney Kyte, or maybe Roy Fox – would play until dawn.

Thus the first shoot at Worlds End was a great success and worth all the labour involved. I cannot recall all the guests shooting, but some names come to mind who were certainly guests at Eaton, but maybe not at Worlds End that first shoot: Lord Portal, Lord Rochdale, Sir Joseph Laycock, Colonel Leslie, Mr Ikey Bell and of course Mr W. Churchill, as he then was. Mr Churchill was a frequent visitor to Eaton. I recall one occasion when I was carrying cartridges for His Grace and Mr Churchill was the next gun in the line. Mr Churchill shot the first cock pheasant that morning, and His Grace turned to me and ordered, "Pull the tail feather out of that bird and stick it in Winnie's hat." With some hesitation I approached Mr Churchill and during a lull in the shooting said, "Excuse me, sir. His Grace has told me to put this feather in your hat." His face beamed and he replied "You do that then, lad," bending over to make it easier for me to do so. I don't know if you would call that a feather in my cap, but it was certainly one in Mr Churchill's.

Mr Churchill was without doubt one of the guns at Worlds End, and if memory serves me well he had been involved in an accident whilst in a taxi in New York. He was still a bit shaky and, with quite an amount of walking from one stand to another, a donkey had been laid on to transport him. A large number of the stands were inaccessible by vehicle and a donkey was considered most suitable, being easier to get on and off than a pony. All went well, and Mr Churchill with the help of his loader managed to dismount and in fact shot very well, that is, until the last drive of the day when he flatly refused to dismount. Instead he demanded that the loader give him a gun and he would shoot from the donkey's back! Fortunately the donkey had by now become used to the barrage at each rise, and with the handler sticking firmly by the donkey's head Mr Churchill proceeded to shoot, accounting for quite a number of birds! I only wish a photograph had been taken of this unusual incident – it must be unique in the history of pheasant shooting. Later in the 1930s Mr Churchill appeared to be deep in thought, often letting many birds go over him without taking the slightest notice. He was by pre-war standards a good though not an excellent shot, but he was a great gentleman who will never be forgotten.

The end of the season at Worlds End left a lot of pheasants on the ground, and it was decided to have a day's shooting for the loaders and local farmers. The day itself was a great success, but I'm afraid the number of birds killed was not very large. The shooting was a bit wild, being at the end of the season, and hardly up to the standard of His Grace's guests. Such days are always looked forward to by the people concerned and are what I suppose you could call a "public relations" job.

After another reason at Worlds End, shooting was again to take place at Eaton. The lease had some time to run but no matter – His Grace had decided to shoot again at home, and shooting at Eaton it had to be. I had to return to the low country, and this time lodgings had been arranged for me at Poulton with Harry Morgan, who at that time was the guard on the private railway. Poulton was about two miles from the Hall and on the beat I was to take over.

6

Poulton, where I was now in lodgings, was next to the Eaton–Pulford drive, which ran a distance of three miles or so. Eaton Hall itself is almost in the centre of the Estate, with five drives radiating from it like the spokes of a wheel. Unfortunately some of the drives are now closed, and although the drive-side woods are well maintained, the drives themselves are rather neglected – once again the reason is the massive amount of money needed to maintain an estate the size of Eaton. The main drives are in very good order and give access to all main points, Chester, Wrexham, and Whitchurch.

My arrival at Poulton coincided with His Grace's wish to establish a new rise on the Pulford drive, the scene of my introduction to pheasant shooting. My beat extended from the Hall to Pulford and included the Serpentine, a large stretch of water covering about eighty acres and near the aptly-named Duck Wood with its pigeon shooting. The beat had been well keepered for many years, so it had a good coverage of tunnel traps and was comparatively free of vermin. Tom Starks, Dick's son, had been the keeper on the beat and he introduced me to the several farmers on the patch. Farmers must be on the side of the keeper, otherwise things can get a bit awkward. Fortunately at Eaton most farms had been in the same family for several generations, so the farmers were well versed with the keeper's activities, even if they themselves were not keen on shooting. Most of them were, though! As a matter of fact, the Eaton farms that are still farmed by tenant farmers are held by the same families that were here fifty years ago. Several families have died out and the land is now taken over by the vast Home Farm.

During the last war, part of the parkland and several farms were taken over as an emergency landing strip for the R.A.F., creating a vast open space on the old Pulford beat. The runways are still there and have proved useful to the present Duke, the 6th; being young, modern and up-to-date, he has had various light aircraft and now uses a helicopter regularly. Although the old runways cover a good many acres with concrete, the rest of the land is used for agriculture, and with good hard standing for vehicles is an ideal site for various country events. Several point-to-point meetings are held there every year by local hunts, and show jumping in the summer. A couple of times under the 5th Duke's auspices there were coach-driving trials, when we were honoured by H.R.H. Prince Philip taking part.

So there have been many changes over the years, but when I first came to Poulton the main activity was shooting, mostly pheasants. For several weeks I spent most of my time finding my way around, looking at the numerous tunnel traps regularly. In the course of my travels I made it my business to have a few words with any farm worker I came across, and I found them to be most helpful, having no doubt been well treated by Tom Starks in the past.

One day Dick Starks and Sandy Myles, the Head Forester, came and there was much discussion over what was needed to create, as His Grace wished, a new rise. It was decided that a section of the drive-side would be most suitable, where the birds could be driven back home to the Young Wood. This would require some work from the woodmen, both to create a flushing point and to make some room for some of the guns to stand. This second problem was more difficult as it entailed felling several mature trees, and His Grace did not like to see trees felled. Sandy Myles decided he might get away with it if the job was done when the Duke was not in residence. This eventually was done, and although His Grace said nothing I bet he knew what had happened.

On one occasion when we were round some farms after snipe, the Duke stopped dead in his tracks and, turning to Fred Milton, his loader, said, "What has happened to the tree that stood by those

79

farm buildings?" Fred didn't know so he was told to find out, and it transpired that it had to be taken down because it was becoming a danger to the buildings. I suppose the Duke was satisfied with the explanation. Not only were there several more trees around the farm but more remarkably, the Duke had not been in that particular area for several years!

The work on the new rise was completed and it was decided that it would not be wired round: the pheasants would be put in the Young Wood and drawn out to the new spot by feeding. This is not always an easy thing to achieve, but with diligence and know-how usually proves satisfactory. Despite my two years at Worlds End under the watchful eye of Tom Lamont, this was obviously a challenge to me but one to which I really looked forward, knowing full well that Dick Starks would be around to guide me.

The birds were reared in the usual manner and eventually arrived at the Young Wood. The weather was kind that summer — long, dry, hot days, which was a great help. The Young Wood, being on clay, could be very wet and wet conditions in those days usually meant "gapes" in the poults, for which there was no cure (today an antidote is readily available). The birds grew well and about mid-September, when they started to stray, the time had arrived to feed them at the new rise. Dick Starks, who had been ailing for some time, now had to be driven about by George Astbury in a car provided by the Duke. Dick often came to see how things were going but was less active and seldom walked more than a hundred yards or so from the car. He gave me several good pieces of advice, and by November when the shoot approached a good number of birds were feeding in the right places.

The big day arrived, the weather was kind and, despite nervous butterflies in my stomach, all was well. The birds flew just as planned, providing good sport for the Duke and his guests. I could see by Dick's face as he stood with the guns that it had been a success, and to my surprise Fred, who was loading for the Duke, beckoned me to him when the drive was over. His Grace shook hands, which was unusual, and thanked me for a job well done. That was a great encouragement and made my day. The number of birds killed does not really matter, but it was considerable and all provided excellent sport.

At the end of that season Dick Starks' health was failing and the next year, after being in hospital for some time, he passed away. His Grace attended the funeral in Eccleston Church, the Grosvenor family church, and a good many people lost a true friend, me amongst them.

It was decided that a new Head Keeper would not be appointed, but that Fred Milton, the Duke's loader, would be foreman on the Park half of the Estate and George Grass foreman at Aldford, where the second day of the two-day shoots took place. Sandy Myles, the Head Forester, a keen shooting man, was to be overall in charge, and the paperwork involved done at his office.

With the Serpentine and Duck Wood on my beat, there were eight hundred to a thousand ducks to be reared annually. It was part of my duties to feed these wildfowl and to look after them generally. The Duke was quite keen on shooting wildfowl but rarely had an organised shoot, preferring to go out often alone, and often at very short notice. Ducks were quite easy to rear even then (more so today) under broody hens and near good water. Once the ducklings reach the age of about fourteen days they can be allowed on the water and need little attention other than feeding, even just once a day. Under fourteen days of age the ducklings lack the oil in their feathers which they normally get from the mother duck, and if allowed onto deep water would drown. It sounds Irish, a duck drowning, but it is true in this context. At six weeks the ducklings were taken to a small, wired-in section on the Serpentine, part water and part land, where they were fed regularly. At this stage they could almost fly, so it wasn't long before they were flying over the wire and onto the Serpentine itself, where they were completely free. A lovely sight are young ducks, swimming in long lines on a beautiful stretch of sun-dappled water. There were plenty of pike in the water, but the ducks were now a bit too big for even the largest predatory fish.

The Serpentine is still full of fish of various sorts and on one occasion when the Game Department did some netting of small fish to re-stock a river (the Yorkshire Ouse, if I remember right) a lot of pike were taken out, the largest weighing nineteen and a half pounds. A pike of around the thirty-pound mark was caught many years ago by a Teddy Wells who worked in the Estate Office. This fish was at one time on display in the Grosvenor Museum in Chester, so I assume it was the largest pike caught in the area at that time.

Talking of fishing brings to mind an incident in the local pub at Aldford. A certain gardener, a keen fisherman, had that evening been fishing in Aldford brook, close to the hostelry. Cyril, the gardener, was prone to exaggeration over most things, but when talking about fishing was at his best. This evening he had caught

what must have been a big fish, a perch I believe, and was describing at great lengths the fight the fish had put up. He finished in the traditional manner by extending his arms to almost full stretch. George Astbury and I were listening to Cyril's glowing description of the evening's exploit and George, also a keen fisherman, who had spent all his youth at the local water mill, could stand it no longer. Always ready for a laugh and pretty good at exaggeration himself, George said, "You've never seen a tidy fish, Cyril." He then told about the time his father took him fishing as a lad one Sunday morning at a lake at Bolesworth Castle, about three miles across country from the mill smallholding. After walking across the fields soon after dawn, George's father set his line up and cast into the lake. George, as lads will, rambled off when the fish showed no signs of biting. He was some distance away when he heard an urgent shout from his father: "Come here, lad, I've got a good 'un!" George rushed back to his father, who was hauling on a very tight line, and helped to pull the fish to the bank. In George's words, "It was such a monster that when we got it on dry land, the lake went down a foot!" Cyril stood open-mouthed, and without a word or even stopping to drain his glass, left the pub in great haste. This was country leg-pulling at its best.

His Grace would only shoot the ducks three or four times a year, and this was really a simple operation. He would walk through the Duck Wood, across a field to the edge of the water where there was a permanent hide. The keepers had two jobs to do. Some were responsible for putting the ducks in the air, which was done by walking down each side of the Serpentine with as little noise as possible. His Grace did not like man-made noises when out shooting so that made the operation more difficult than it might have been. Waving a handkerchief and rattling a half-full match-box often did the trick, but care had to be taken not to put too many of the wildfowl into the air at once, or the shooting period would be shorter than His Grace wanted. The rest of the keepers always remained in the Duck Wood; these were the dog men, whose job was to pick up all the birds shot. A boat was available but used only if the numbers lying dead on the water would have taxed the stamina of all the dogs present. At certain times there would be a very large number of birds on the water, comprising many species of duck, but the Duke rarely shot anything but mallard and seemed able to pick that breed out even in flight.

For this reason, and because there were rarely more than two or three guns, no large numbers of ducks were killed. Around a hundred head was quite a good bag, which since the shooting only lasted about an hour may be considered very satisfactory.

I do recall one incident when duck shooting on the Serpentine. His Grace had a guest with him, who was handicapped in some respect and sat on his shooting stick throughout. This was unusual but did happen on occasions. What was really extraordinary was that this gentleman was using not a shotgun but a .22 repeating rifle. Imagine shooting flying ducks with a rifle! Nor was this all, for he did not even put the rifle to his shoulder — he shot from the hip. With the butt of the rifle at his hip and his right hand in the correct position, he was able to bring down quite a number of birds in full flight! I may possibly be wrong but memory seems to say it was the Lord Rochdale of that time.

On another occasion the 2nd Duke's daughter, Lady Mary Grosvenor, was shooting duck on the Serpentine and I was honoured to load for her. Unfortunately the pair of guns she was using were hammer guns, non-ejector, and not conducive to the rapid changing of guns. Ducks were quite plentiful, but I was not sorry that there were fewer than sometimes. Lady Mary was very understanding, realising the difficulties of a loader with hammer guns, and quite recently, when I was again loading for her Ladyship at a pheasant shoot, recalled that day after ducks.

The lake below the Hall, the Fishpond, always had a large stock of waterfowl of all descriptions, some of which were ornamental species. His Grace would never shoot this piece of water, preferring to be able to see the birds on the water when he took a stroll around the lovely gardens, as he frequently did when in residence.

Snipe shooting round the marl pits was a sport His Grace was very fond of, as I had discovered during my first week at Eaton, and he seldom took another gun with him on these expeditions. "Going round the pits" was a simple operation which often entailed a lot of walking but only involved two keepers and of course Fred Milton who always loaded for the Duke. The Duke always used two guns, even when snipe shooting, but no matter if twenty ducks or teal got off the pit, His Grace would not even raise his gun until a snipe moved. I suppose he was rather eccentric over this, as most people would shoot at ducks when put up, but not the Duke. Remarkably, be it pheasants, ducks, snipe or woodcock he was after, that was all he would ever pull trigger at.

George Astbury, as driver to the Game Department, was responsible for getting Fred and the keepers to the appointed spot. A trailer for the Armstrong Siddeley car had been specially built, and the dogs and other essentials travelled on this. Once the route round the pits had been decided, George and the Duke's chauffeur would take the cars to the pick-up spot and await the arrival of the shooting party. Sometimes it might be a long wait. Snipe are not

easy targets, being very small birds and having a habit of zig-
zagging away at a remarkable turn of speed when flushed from a
pit. They do have the tendency to sit very tight, often until a dog
almost treads on them, which makes it possible to get quite a
number of shots at any one pit. His Grace, an excellent shot, took
full advantage of this and, unless a whole "wisp" of snipe got off a
pit, usually accounted for a good number on every trip out. I have
seen him kill four birds with four rapid shots, having changed
guns with Fred.

One problem was picking the snipe up when they had been shot.
If they fell on the open field it wasn't so bad but often they would
fall in the rushes surrounding the pond. These birds needed very
good dogs to retrieve them, as snipe do not carry a lot of scent and
are not very attractive to a dog.

Most of the dogs used at Eaton in those days were black
labradors, as the yellow only became popular much later. Several
keepers had flat-coated retrievers, dogs seldom seen these days, but
I had at that time a black, curly-coated retriever called Sam. He
was particularly good at finding snipe, or for that matter almost
anything, so I frequently had the job of remaining behind at a pit
to find any snipe that hadn't been picked up. I remember once, at a
pit which was particularly good for snipe and had a large area of
the type of rush the birds favoured, having to remain behind to
find a jack snipe. Everyone thought that all the birds brought down
had been accounted for, but the Duke was insistent that one still
remained and that it was a jack snipe. This variety of snipe is the
smallest of the breed and not easy to find on grassland, let alone in
thick rushes. A couple of dogs had hunted the pit pretty well,
picking up several birds, and of course this made it less easy for
Sam. However he started working the pit systematically, as good
dogs will, and after about ten minutes started to scratch away at the
rushes until the mud underneath started to fly. Eventually he poked
his nose down into the mud and his tail started to wag. Then he
straightened himself up and picked his way to me with his head in
the air and his muzzle covered in mud. I opened his mouth and
there was a snipe – a jack snipe at that! His Grace was very
pleased, but to his credit he did not say, "I told you so."

During the 1930s many trips were made round the pits in search
of snipe. It was possible to go out every day of a week and not visit
the same pit twice, but His Grace did this only once in my time,
and his target was one hundred snipe. This objective was reached,
and little more snipe shooting was done that season.

Large areas of boggy land on the Estate, such as withy beds, also
attracted snipe. One in particular covered at least 150 acres, part of

84

which was completely open. This naturally made it a favourite spot for snipe. The method used on this type of ground involved more keepers than when going round the pits, and sometimes the Duke would have a guest or two with him – maybe his agent, Major Basil Kerr, or another local gentleman. Butts had been built many years previously, and access to these was via a raised row of planks, like a pier. Once the guns were in position the keepers would drive the area in the hope of putting the snipe over the waiting shooting party. Snipe are almost impossible to drive, but with the butts cunningly placed, quite a proportion of the birds flushed would go over them. Driven snipe are a completely different target from those flushed off a pit, but being small birds give excellent sport. Quite a number were often killed, and of course this type of shooting did not entail too much walking.

I have already mentioned that the 2nd Duke was rather eccentric. There was the time when shooting the withy beds that he arrived wearing one riding boot and one wellington, but of course no remark was passed about this. I recall another time when he was due to be out shooting at 10.30 am. It was a bitter cold day, the wind blowing half a gale from the east. Four of us keepers were in position to drive the beds by 10.15, and by the very nature of the land were in an exposed position. Time went on but no sign of the Duke, eleven o'clock, twelve o'clock, but still no signal to proceed. Midday passed and by now we were all frozen to the marrow but dared not move. At 2.45 Sandy Myles appeared on the skyline and signalled to us to go to him, which we were only too pleased to do. It transpired that the Duke's instructions had been misunderstood and that he had just left for London in the Rolls!

On another occasion in those same withy beds, and again driving the snipe, there was more than the usual amount of water about. The planks which crossed the ditches were about six inches below the surface. This wasn't too bad and we all knew where the planks were as we usually followed the same course as we progressed down the bed. There was quite a nice lot of shooting as the birds went forward, and we looked forward to an easier task than usual as the snipe would be on the surface of the water and that much easier to see and retrieve. Eventually the keepers came to within sight of the Duke and his guest, with one more line of planks to cross before the picking up started. All crossed safely with the exception of Jim Saint. We heard a roar of laughter from His Grace and looked round. Of Jim there was no sign! All that could be seen was his hard hat, with his dog swimming to retrieve it. Jim had slid silently off the plank and for a short while was completely submerged. It wasn't a laughing matter really as we were all wearing waders and poor old Jim had some difficulty clambering out to shallow water. He was like a drowned rat, but the retrieving of the dead snipe was soon completed. On arriving at the cars, the Duke as he always did thanked us all, and then turned to Sandy Myles and said, "Take them all to the Grosvenor Arms," (the village pub) "and get some whisky. We can't have Jim catching a death of cold." It was during closing hours, but Sandy soon raised the landlady and we settled down by a blazing fire and carried out the Duke's orders! Jim was soon steaming but escaped without a chill. Hardy chaps, those old-time gamekeepers.

Snipe must be a delicacy, for the 2nd Duke seemed very fond of them and often, when he was going to London, the keepers had to get some to go with him. Most times when he was in residence, a supply of them was maintained in the game larder at the Hall, but on several occasions the keepers were caught on the hop. A telephone message would be received at the Kennels to the effect that the Duke needed some snipe to take to London and would be leaving on the 10.40 am from Crewe. Crewe was about an hour by road, so if the message was received about half past eight, it didn't leave a lot of time to get eight or ten of the little, long-billed birds. George Astbury was the key figure in this urgent operation, being the only one of the staff able to drive a car. A couple of keepers would jump into the car and be driven off to a spot that always held snipe, other keepers would go to ponds near the Kennels, and with the short time available no-one could afford to miss many shots. I don't remember the Duke ever being disappointed.

When the Duke was in residence during the shooting season, keepers always had to be at hand in case they were needed. If no message had been received at the Kennels by about ten in the morning, it was the custom for Fred Milton and one other keeper to go to the Hall, just in case the Duke decided to go for a quick walk round a pit or two. One day when it was my turn to go with Fred, we had waited some time and in fact were having lunch in the servants' hall when the butler informed us that the Duke would be out shortly to go for a shot or two. He wanted to go to "Radley Meadow", a partially flooded field that did attract snipe. For once, which was most out of character, he decided to drive himself in a Ford V8, a staff car really. We all got in, His Grace drove right down to the meadow and several snipe were shot. On getting back to the car the Duke said, "That was great fun. It will do for today." So far so good, but after travelling only a short distance the car became bogged down in the deeply rutted lane. There was nothing for it but Fred and myself to get out and push. Push we did, but they were heavy cars in those days and it took considerable effort to get the vehicle onto a solid surface. We got back in and the Duke thanked us for our efforts. Next morning, at the crack of dawn, contractors arrived to make a good surface on the lane. It is still a good sound road, but to the best of my knowledge the Duke never went down that lane again!

On our way back to the Hall that day, we had to pass the Grosvenor Arms. The Duke slowed up, but I couldn't see him calling for a drink! However, the reason for slowing up soon became evident because lo and behold, the rector of the parish was standing on the steps! The Duke wound the window down, and with a grin on his face shouted, "I've caught you this time you old b———!" No doubt it was taken in good part by the Rev. Paddy Austin, a real sporting parson who was particularly fond of hunting.

There are not so many snipe about now. This is due to a variety of circumstances, I suppose, but there is no doubt in my mind that the basic reason is the drastic change in the environment. Many of the old-time favourite pits are now badly overgrown, with tall rushes right to the edge. The cattle used to keep the surrounds of a pond well trodden, but with water troughs in every field they no longer do so. The water meadows are much better drained, leaving only small patches as suitable feeding grounds for the long-billed snipe. Seldom in this area of Cheshire does one hear the snipe "drumming", a sure sign of a nest not too far away.

Another long-billed bird is the woodcock, which owes its popularity with most shooting men to the difficult target it presents as it flits rapidly through the trees when once disturbed. Being a dappled brown, it is most difficult to see even when airborne as it passes through the similar shades of the autumn woodlands. Many sportsmen are proud to have a woodcock pin feather or two in their hat-band, a sign of their prowess with a gun. At one time it was possible to earn a bottle of liqueur from a well-known purveyor of wines and spirits by killing a right-and-left at woodcock – a right-and-left at snipe will earn the same prize to this day.

His Grace was a keen woodcock shot and would often spend a few hours in pursuit of this elusive bird. The usual procedure was for several keepers to drive a wood whilst the Duke stood in a spot that the woodcock were likely to pass. Once we were driving a wood called the "Glebe" and quite a number of woodcock were about. His Grace had had several shots but we knew that some of the birds we had flushed had not gone over him, for they have a habit of flying so far and then settling again. As we came quite close to where the Duke was standing, another bird rose into the air. Bang! The Duke had shot at it and I saw it fall to the ground. It wasn't only the woodcock that had been shot, though, and old Ted Milton appeared with blood running down his cheek. The Duke asked, "What's the matter, Ted?" and Ted replied, "You've shot 'ee, 'ee Grace." This was very upsetting to the Duke, who was always so particular over safety with guns, but it was obvious that one pellet had caught Ted as it ricocheted off either a tree or a thick bough. The Duke could not apologise enough and finished by saying, "What will it be Ted, old chap, whisky or champagne?" Ted answered promptly, "Whisky, please, 'ee Grace." That evening the Duke's private secretary arrived at Ted's cottage, not with a bottle of whisky but with a case of whisky – and for good measure a case of champagne!

Fortunately there have been very, very few cases of people being shot during my fifty years as a keeper at Eaton. In fact no-one has actually been shot, but there have been several minor accidents when a deflected pellet has drawn blood. I have a pellet in my leg which has been there almost forty years, having been deflected off a hard road whilst we were driving for rabbits. It is amazing how far a pellet like that will travel; I must have been at least two hundred yards away, yet it penetrated a box-cloth legging and lodged in my leg. It stung a bit at the time but there has been no discomfort since.

Other minor accidents have of course happened in the shooting field at Eaton and Mr Churchill was involved in one of these, sometime around the mid-1930s. I was not actually present but his regular loader, Heber Fearnall, told us all about it. Most guests brought a shooting stick on the big shoots to sit on should there be a wait. This time there was a lull in the shooting and Mr Churchill promptly sat down on his shooting stick, gun still in hand. A few seconds later the stick snapped in half and "Winnie" was on his

backside on the ground! Most sticks were of cane in those days, so it appears that Mr Churchill suffered somewhat from rot. His gun went flying, and although loaded it was on safe so it did not fire, but Winnie was not the slightest bit amused. After being helped to his feet, he asked Heber to hand him the broken stick and, having examined it, he walked about twenty yards and threw the pieces into the close-by pond. No doubt the metal parts are still lying there, rusting away in the mud. Once Mr Churchill recovered from the shock he obviously saw the humorous side of it and said, "That would have made a good cartoon!" Then he looked around to see if any cameras had been clicking, but he was safe there as no photographs were ever taken at an actual shoot without permission.

Pheasants falling from a great height can be a hazard, and I recall two accidents that could have been serious. One, in the distant past, was when a bird had been killed at great height and fell straight onto the guest who had shot it. The bird caught him on the right forearm, dragging his finger through the trigger guard as he was about to fire another shot. The gun went off harmlessly into the air, but the gentleman's finger was quite badly lacerated and needed medical attention. He only missed one rise, but I don't suppose he shot quite so well for the rest of the day.

Quite recently a similar thing happened at Aldford. The

Torment rise always provides good high birds and one of the guns, the Duke of Abercorn, was caught in a similar situation, but this time the pheasant hit him full in the face, knocking him to the ground. A badly bruised face and two black eyes were the result, and unfortunately he had to retire from the day's sport. A well-fed pheasant can weigh three or four pounds, and falling from a hundred feet or so can give one a fair clout.

For many, many years wild geese have been visitors to the water meadows at Eaton, some of which flood during the winter months. Pre-war all of these birds were winter visitors, consisting mainly of white-fronts with a sprinkling of pink-feet. Today nearly all the geese are resident Canadas. Colonel Gerald Grosvenor, before he became the 4th Duke, introduced thirty goslings from Lord Cholmondeley's estate at Cholmondeley, about six miles away as the crow flies. These goslings were pinioned and put on the Serpentine. Several were killed by foxes but now, after about twenty-five years, quite large numbers have built up, and they fly frequently to Cholmondeley and Carden, another estate several miles away. They breed in the area, often on the pits where formerly the snipe were to be found, and it is to be hoped that they do not become too numerous. Geese grazing on winter-sown corn or even on grass-land can cause considerable damage, and so are unpopular with the farming community.

Colonel Robert Grosvenor, who became the 5th Duke on the death of the 4th Duke, his brother, in 1967, was very keen on wildfowl both wild and ornamental. At his request and with the help and co-operation of the Wildfowlers' Association (W.A.G.B.I.), greylag geese were introduced. The first lot of goslings, about two dozen as I remember, were brought down from a good breeding area in Scotland and released on the Fishpond in the gardens. This operation was not a great success, since many were killed by foxes and most of the others were driven away by the numerous Canada geese on the water. The following year, eggs almost on the point of hatching came from the same source and were successfully hatched and reared. When the goslings were released they were able to fly, so were much better equipped to survive; a few have been reared each year for several years and a good number are now resident and breeding on the estate. The last estimate was in excess of eighty birds, so after consultation with Mr John Richards of W.A.G.B.I. it was decided that no further rearing was needed. The greylag is a much nicer goose than the Canada, and since it tends to feed in small groups, less damage is done to agricultural land. It is hoped the greylag will gradually oust the Canada at Eaton, as has happened elsewhere.

Geese are not often shot inland in Cheshire, but a few are shot on the Dee estuary and Frodsham marshes. They are a pretty wily bird in the wild state. Of course there is a saying, "A wild goose chase", and how true that is. It is almost impossible to get anywhere near them on the ground, and when in the air they seem to sense the slightest unusual thing and soon take evasive action to avoid it. The sound they make when flying over my cottage on their way to the feeding grounds is a joy to hear, and it is possible even to pick out the call of one individual goose that I suppose has passed over hundreds of times. It is music to the ear when they go over, especially on a moonlit night. I can stand a lot of that sort of "noise", much better than heavy lorries passing or even, dare I say it, the television!

Sandy Myles was very keen on shooting when he took charge of the Game Department after the death of Dick Starks, but it was patently obvious that he was far from fully aware of the ins and outs of the job. Several things proved that, but I should like to tell about the goose. George Astbury and I were talking to him on a winter afternoon when a skein of geese went over, honking their way to the water meadows. Sandy remarked on them and said that he had never tasted one. When he asked if it would be possible to get one, George said it would before I could warn him that in my experience a wild goose will usually be tough to the point of being inedible.

Knowing one particular area where the geese went to feed at eventide, we decided to be there at dusk and await their arrival. Sure enough, as the light was fading a large skein of probably two hundred or more white-fronts could be seen high in the sky, approaching from the north. They passed over me completely out of range and vanished into the distance. George shouted from his hiding place that they looked like going elsewhere that evening, but of course geese don't just make one dive onto their feeding grounds; they usually pass over and assess any possible danger first. It was some time before we could hear their familiar gabbling, approaching again from the south-west. This time they were much lower, but when they arrived they were still out of range of our twelve-bore guns. Keeping perfectly still, we let them pass over us, and as they swung round and disappeared once more into the night sky, I could see they were now getting much lower. Soon I could hear them approaching yet again, but this time the honking was interspersed with much cackling, a sure sign that they were about to land. I wondered who would be able to get a shot at them, and soon realised that although I could not see them, they were much nearer to George than to me. Suddenly, all the noise they were making ceased and almost that second there were two shots in quick succession, followed by a dull thud. George had managed to knock one down. The geese then made a terrific din, and their wings could be heard thrashing the air as they beat a hasty retreat to pastures new. George soon appeared out of the gathering gloom, carrying one large goose, and sure enough it was a white-front which must have weighed at least six pounds. Sandy Myles would be pleased!

It was now early evening, but George said we may as well deliver the bird direct to Sandy, as it was not much out of our way. When we arrived, the look of surprise on Sandy's face made it obvious that he had not expected us to get a goose so quickly. He soon produced the whisky bottle and said how delighted he was, then told us what he proposed to do with the bird: he would get it plucked and dressed, put an onion inside, and then hang it in his larder for a fortnight. This should impart a good flavour to it, according to what he had heard. After another nip or two of whisky (in fact there wasn't much left in the bottle by then), we left.

I suppose it must have been three weeks later, when Sandy was at the Kennels to discuss some matter, that George asked him, "What was the goose like, boss?" Sandy, with a dour look on his face, said "Ach, laddie, dinna talk to me about geese. That one was so tough, we couldn't chew the gravy." This caused a certain amount of merriment amongst the assembled keepers but Sandy obviously wasn't very amused.

It is said you should never shoot the first few leading geese in a skein but try and get one bringing up the rear. I don't know what truth there is in this but I would have thought that one bringing up the rear could just as easily be a very old, feeble bird trying to keep up with the rest. Probably one reason why comparatively few geese are shot, apart from their wildness, is the fact that only a very young bird can be guaranteed to be tender. The question is how do you pick a young bird out? A great friend of mine, Frank Mossford, who still has a very large collection of ornamental wild-fowl, once shot and pinioned a greylag goose, which recovered and took its place in his goose pen. It was a goose, and eventually paired with a hand-reared gander, but Frank had it for twenty-three years before it layed an egg! So how old are some of the geese that visit us in winter? No wonder Sandy Myles couldn't chew the gravy. One thing – he never asked us to get him another one.

7

My beat at Poulton ran up to the Welsh border, in fact part of it was in Denbighshire as it was in those days. Being not too far from Wrexham, we inevitably suffered from a certain amount of poaching. Several coal mines in the Wrexham area were bound to provide some poachers, for it was well known that colliers were the mainstay of the poaching community. Worlds End had been practically free of any poaching, but now at Poulton I was to become involved with men bent on their nefarious business. Poaching has been going on since time immemorial, but it increases at times of shortage of money and work, as in the depressed mid-1930s.

The old-time poaching fraternity were a very different class of men to those engaged in the pursuit today. Walking or biking often for many miles, the old hands were quite content with a few rabbits, since in any case a man is limited by the number of conies he can carry plus the tackle needed to catch them. Maybe fifteen rabbits made a heavy enough load, so no fortunes were made poaching; rabbits at about tenpence a couple did not provide a large sum after a night's work, even if you weren't caught.

There was of course poaching and poaching, and often there would be the local man who would sneak out and get a couple of rabbits to feed the family, or the farm labourer who would hit one

94

with a stick when he came across it in its "seat" in the open field. Those who took the largest number of rabbits nearly always came from further afield, but no matter where they came from it was the keepers' duty to catch as many as possible. The farm worker's thieving was more or less ignored, as long as it happened on the farm where he worked, but the keeper usually made sure that the man knew that the keeper knew, so that the farm man did not get any ideas about taking a pheasant or two! The cottager who snared or ferreted the odd rabbit to feed the family often got the reputation of being a poacher on the grand scale, mostly by boasting in the local pub and telling tales of how he had evaded the keepers, but as a rule these small-timers were easily caught. They naturally did not tell about those times in the pubs, but at Eaton several were dealt with over the years and the general public never got to know.

The 2nd Duke was averse to publicity of any sort, and gave instructions that poachers were not to be prosecuted unless they had assaulted any of the keepers. The keepers naturally had to take some action, otherwise the Estate would have been overrun by these "sportsmen", so it was the custom to deal with any poachers caught in the following fashion. Names and addresses were always taken and no matter what "engine of destruction" they were using it was confiscated, be it net, snare, ferret or gun. They were then instructed to pay one pound to their nearest hospital and forward the receipt to the Head Keeper within a month. This seemed to work wonderfully well, and I don't remember a single poacher failing to provide a receipt. I suppose they preferred to do it our way than appear in court and suffer the publicity, even if it did overall cost them a bit more.

Fortunately we were not too pestered with pheasant poaching at that time but later, when more motor-cars came onto the roads, a certain amount did go on and for that matter is still going on. There were literally thousands of rabbits all over the Estate, so I suppose in a way the poachers were helping to keep them down, but I don't know a keeper who could allow this state of affairs to carry on without trying to catch some of the offenders.

Most of the visitors after rabbits came at night with the intention of long netting. The long net is a net of varying length but normally of either fifty or a hundred yards, the fifty-yard one being favoured by poachers as it could be carried easily in a "poacher's pocket" (a large pocket inside the jacket, which also had a long narrow pocket to carry the pegs to set the net). Two men could set two hundred yards of netting along a wood and with the number of rabbits often out feeding, it did not take long to catch as many as they could carry. So it was important from the keeper's point of view to be in the right place at the right time.

The Poulton beat was pretty well wooded, having a wide wood the full length of the Pulford drive, a total distance of two and a half miles. This gave a wide range of places to set a long net and made it possible for rabbits to be netted on almost any suitable night. All the same, there were things that could be done to check the long netting of rabbits – tricks little used these days, as with fewer rabbits about there is almost no long netting done. Outside most of the woods where the bulk of the pheasants roosted it was the custom to place "bushes", branches cut from hawthorn or blackthorn, and sometimes even short lengths of rusty barbed wire, that tearing memento of the First World War. It is easy to imagine the chaos if a lightweight hemp net is run across a particularly spiky thorn bough. The nets were usually run out by one man and pegged at about five-yard intervals by the other before the rabbits were driven in, so the disturbance caused by untangling the net from the thorns put the rabbits back in the wood. This ruse meant that most night visitors kept away from the pheasant woods, having no doubt learned by bitter experience that there was little to gain by going there. Over such a vast area it was of course possible to bush only selected places, but at least it did narrow the field of operations a bit and perhaps reduced the temptation to take a pheasant or two.

My first experience of poachers was at Aldford, although I was on the Poulton beat. Early September was often the time long netting started; in fact as soon as the ground was soft enough to get the necessary pegs in, you could be sure that the poachers would be after rabbits. This particular year, word had been received on the grapevine that poachers might be coming to net partridge. Partridges can be netted by using a drag net, that is a net approximately fifteen yards square, with fairly long drag lines. The net is drawn across a field where partridges are known to be spending the night, and as soon as the covey is heard to take off the net is dropped, trapping the little brown bird beneath. With large coveys of hand-reared partridge on most fields at Aldford at that time, it was particularly vulnerable to this type of poaching, and in view of the information received a full night-time watch was to be kept on the area. Some of us keepers from the park were helping George Grass in this security operation, so there were very few hours of darkness when it could be poached with immunity.

The night I met my first poachers was quite a windy one, and a windy night is essential for netting of either partridge or rabbits as on a still night sounds travel a surprising distance. A fellow keeper, Ron Jones, and I had been watching for a couple of hours or so and all was quiet, so we decided to go and meet the other keepers on duty, George Grass and Jack Parsons, at a pre-arranged rendez-vous. So that none of the partridge would be disturbed we did not cross any fields but kept to the hedges and woodsides. When we were only one field away from where we knew George and Jack would be, and just starting up the side of a wood, Ron suddenly fell to the ground. He didn't shout but just whispered, "A net!" He had stumbled over a long net, ready set to catch rabbits!

Now we were in a dilemma: did we whistle to warn George, or did we wait at the net for the poachers to return? After a whispered consultation we decided to wait and we didn't have to wait long. A man appeared in the half-light, coming down the woodside. We were crouched under the hedge as well hidden as possible and, when the poacher came up to us, jumped up right in his path. Surprised, he immediately took to his heels. I snatched my whistle from my pocket as I started after him, but as I put it to my mouth I went flying over the net and nearly swallowed the whistle in the process! Ron managed to get away without fouling the net and I was soon up and following them, blowing my whistle as hard as I could, hoping that George Grass and Jack would be able to cut the poacher off as he was running in their direction. I caught sight of three figures on the skyline which rather puzzled me, knowing that Ron was chasing one man. Who was the third? Being much more active in those days, I gradually overhauled the shadowy forms in front and could now tell that they were heading for a gate on the far side of the field. I was also aware that our rendezvous with George Grass was very close to where the running men were heading. I shouted, "Look out George!" and almost immediately could hear sounds of a scuffle. As I caught up with Ron, he panted, "I think George and Jack have got them" and told me that another poacher had joined the first almost at the moment I was blowing my whistle.

We got to the gateway and found George and Jack there, as well as one man lying on the ground and another leaning against the gate holding his head. It transpired that the two keepers had stepped out into the gateway when the running poachers were within five yards of it, giving them no time to change course. George had grabbed one and Jack the other. In the confusion that ensued, the two poachers had crashed together, one knocking the other out. That stopped their running and poaching for that night! The usual procedure was gone through, names and addresses taken and instructions given. It turned out that they had come on their bikes from Wrexham, some nine miles away, where they both lived on a council estate called Churton Drive. By coincidence, the spot where they were caught was about half a mile from the village of Churton, but they would do no driving of rabbits that night!

That was my first experience of poachers and an exhilarating one it was. As the years went by there were to be many more occasions when the keepers at Eaton came across the "sportsmen of the night". It was not advisable to tackle poachers on your own in those days, any more than it is today, but sometimes it was unavoidable. One evening during late September I was cycling back to my lodgings with a strong breeze blowing. On reaching a hunting wicket on the drive-side, I dismounted and looked over the small gate, half-expecting to find a net set as it was about an hour after dark and a favourite time for the "early brigade". I must have been there about ten minutes when I heard the rustle of footsteps behind me on the drive-side verge. I did not turn round, knowing full well that any movement would give away my presence, but I had been seen. A voice whispered, "There's someone there" and at the same time the footsteps stopped. The rustling in the grass started up again and, after hesitating a while, I turned round and could just see two forms hurrying away. I started to run after them and they at once dashed off at great speed. I lost sight of them in the gloom but continued to run in their direction, coming up to them just as they were about to mount their cycles, which they must have retrieved from the bushes. One was just aboard his machine when I gave him a hefty clout on the shoulder with my stick. He tumbled off the bike and his pal, seeing what was happening, picked up his own cycle and threw it at me. I managed to dodge it, and fell on top of the man on the ground! The man on his feet then rushed at me, but I held my stick in front of me like a bayonet and he ran straight into it. That knocked the stuffing out of him! They both decided enough was enough and when asked their names gave them quite meekly. After disentangling their three long nets from the cycles and gathering up the scattered pegs, I decided that this time I would let them go with a strongly worded warning not to come back again. They had been caught before they had even set their nets, but I was lucky to get off so lightly when tackling two men.

We always had a good grapevine; many people were only too keen to let us know of any poaching activity and of course, a lot of information could be gathered in the local pubs, especially those in villages just off the Estate. The poachers, too, had their lines of communication but it was sometimes possible to hoodwink them by laying a false scent! We knew that three poachers had been coming fairly regularly to a certain area, but despite all our efforts they were not caught. But we knew where they came from and decided the time had come to teach them a lesson. They always visited a local pub before disappearing into the night on their nefarious business, so George Eaton, the keeper who had shot the heron at Worlds End and whose beat was taking the brunt of the poachers' activities, spent a Wednesday evening or two there! George Astbury and I had agreed to keep watch on George Eaton's patch while he was at the local hostelry, but we didn't expect any reaction for the first couple of Wednesday evenings. On the fourth Wednesday of George Eaton's visit to the pub, though, our tactics paid off. At about 9 pm three figures approached on cycles and, in accordance with our plan, we let them pass. As we did so, we could see that they were laden with the tackle for a night's netting. The reason we let them pass was to enable us to catch them either in the act or laden with their spoils. Now our job was to find where they had hidden their bikes.

We gave the poachers twenty minutes or so, to make sure they had set off on their netting, and then went in search of their transport. This particular drive had quite a lot of large rhododendron bushes and also some huge yew trees, so it was almost certain that the bikes would be hidden amongst these. Sure enough, we eventually found what we were after, deep in a particularly dense bush. Obviously it would be a good idea to move the bikes in case the poachers eluded us, so we carried them some distance to another suitable hiding-place. The time had passed and we guessed it would not be very long before they would be back. The night was exceptionally good for netting rabbits, with a strong wind blowing right into the wood. Under those conditions, and with the coney so numerous in those days, one set could produce as many rabbits as three men could carry. There was only one way into the bush where the cycles had been hidden so George positioned himself out of sight by the drive-side and I got out of sight in the bush. Sure enough, it wasn't long before a rustle could be heard, even above the wind, as three approaching pairs of feet kicked up the dead leaves. The men had to cross the drive and in the better light I could see that they were well laden. As soon as they passed George, he jumped out and shouted and I immediately did the same. Caught in between us, I suppose they thought they were surrounded!

Being taken by surprise and obviously shaken, as well as being handicapped by their load, they showed no sign of fight. They didn't try to escape, and offered no resistance when told to hand over their catch and tackle. They were well laden: five nets, two being practically new, pegs to set the nets, and forty-six rabbits between them! When we asked their names, one of the poachers refused. For a while it looked like trouble, but George was a well-built man and stood up to them, saying "Right. In that case we'll lock you up for the night." It was only about a mile to the house of the local policeman, who fortunately was at home and agreed to lock them up. He did the job properly, taking statements from the men and getting the name of the one who had refused to give it to us. By now it had gone midnight, and after a cup of tea with the policeman we had to return to collect the "bag" for the night. He told us he would let the poachers loose in an hour or so; as I explained earlier, the 2nd Duke would not have them prosecuted, but it was quite legal to lock poachers up for the night and bring them before an occasional court the next day. These men were really lucky in that respect, but it did cost them a pound each and the loss of their nets. George Eaton was fine and pleased the next day, and as far as we know this particular gang did not visit his beat again.

There was so much rabbit poaching during those depressed years in the 1930s that many incidents come to mind. Around this time, with so many rabbits eating their way through valuable grass and corn crops, the farmers were naturally keen to kill as many as possible, but at the same time did not like poachers fetching them – in a way I suppose you could call them a farm crop, even if a rather uncultivated one! Sandy Myles came to me one day and said that two of the farmers were getting concerned about the number of rabbits going onto the land they farmed, an Estate holding. The animals lived in the woodland of Pulford drive and would feed on the farm of the Denson brothers, "Tut" and Frank, at night. Sandy told me that Tut and Frank would help me if I would try and net a few at night, and as the rabbits were eating their grass, Tut and Frank were to have the catch, if any! I decided to bring George to see Tut and Frank, and a plan was made. If the weather was suitable we would try the nets on a Tuesday and Friday for a week or two and see how we went on. This plan turned out to be very successful and many hundreds of rabbits were caught during the first few weeks. There was no sign of poachers while we were out but Tut and Frank, being two very good sports, told me they would help any time if poaching was suspected. I must admit I enjoyed those nights catching rabbits for Tut and Frank, and gained a lot of experience in setting nets in the dark, a job that takes quite a bit of skill which only practice can provide.

We had really thinned the rabbits out, so that they were now getting quite hard to catch in any numbers, but one Friday Frank called at my lodgings and, although we had not planned to go out that night, said he could do with a dozen or so to take to Chester the next day. So the plans were laid, and we hoped we would get enough by setting the nets once. It turned out to be a good netting night and we did get ample rabbits in the one set. George Astbury was with us and thought it was a likely night for us to have some "visitors". We all agreed and put our catch and nets in the cabin to be collected later. The time passed but no-one appeared. All seemed to be quiet and we were ready to call it a night so we loaded up our catch, leaving the nets and pegs in the hut, and made our way in the direction of the brothers' farm. After going a little way, I sensed there was someone about so I hurried ahead and, peeping over a gate, saw a figure in the gloom apparently coming toward the gate. I called George, Tut and Frank to me, and we slipped through the unfastened gate and hid in the adjacent ditch. In a few minutes the figure I had seen came within a few yards of us and we all bobbed up out of the ditch! He must have had the fright of his life.

We knew he would not be on his own so warned him not to call or shout and dragged him into the ditch where we had hidden. It wasn't long before another figure approached and I climbed out of the ditch, giving the call sign used universally by poachers – a "click click" sound twice repeated. He came right up to me, so unaware that anything was amiss that I could hear him humming a popular tune of the day, "South of the Border"! The rest then got out of the ditch and we soon gathered that there were only the two of them. They said that the rabbits they had caught were at the other end of the nets which were still set, so we proceeded to pick up the nets until we came to the heap of conies. Having sent the miscreants on their way, we took stock of our "plunder" – we had thirty-one rabbits in the heap, a good catch, three nets and a bundle of pegs. Tut said he thought there were a lot of pegs for three nets, so he counted them, forty-four. Tut was right – it looked as if there must be another net somewhere. We searched high and low but could not find it, so eventually gave it up as a bad job.

We arrived at the brothers' farm at Poulton with more rabbits than we expected, and more nets and pegs for the collection. As was the custom, a drink and a snack were due before leaving for home. Tut said, "Go and get something from the pantry, Frank. I'll cut the bread." Frank departed, and came back with a tin of sardines. Tut stared at him and said, "Blast you, Frank! You know I dunna like sardines. Go and get that tin of ham," and ham it was for supper that night. Over our meal there was some discussion about the number of pegs we had taken off the poachers, and we all agreed there must be another net somewhere which it might be possible to find come daylight. I said I would make a thorough search the following day or rather, by now, later that day.

After paunching the rabbits, George and I left Tut and Frank to make our way home. George had to travel about a mile along the Pulford drive before turning off to his home, and since I somehow still had a nagging feeling about those extra pegs, I told George I would travel so far with him and do a final check that no-one was around. Some distance down the drive there was a wide opening in the wood called the "Bantam opening", and at the far side of the opening a hunting wicket giving easy access to the field beyond. The opening itself held a huge oak tree under which grew a dense holly bush, and I had in the past seen signs of poachers using the holly bush to hide their cycles. As we reached the opening I suggested to George, "That holly bush might be worth looking at," so he held my bike whilst I crossed the opening to investigate. I don't know why, but as I approached the bush I gave the call sign used earlier in the night and to my great surprise it was answered from the middle of the holly bush!

George had heard the answering call and rushed across to join me. Out of the bush appeared two figures, one of whom straight-away started to hum "South of the Border". They were the same men we had caught several hours earlier! One of them had a blood-stained piece of cloth wrapped around one hand, and he told us he had cut his hand badly whilst cutting more pegs in the dark. George pushed into the bush and sure enough came out with a net and some rough pegs. Further investigation revealed thirteen rabbits and on counting the pegs later, we found there were thirteen of them – unlucky for some! For sheer cheek this episode takes some beating and with the audacity of it still in our minds we decided to take no further action but sent "South of the Border" and his friend packing. They came from a colliery area, Llay, near Wrexham, some eight miles away, so they would not be too happy to return home without a rabbit, without their nets or pegs but with a cut hand to show for covering sixteen miles and spending several hours roaming around in the dark!

These two men were caught several times after this incident and the really amazing part was that they always answered to the poachers' call sign. Most poachers would do so, but you didn't always catch them! We could never understand why they didn't alter the sign of recognition, but several years later, whilst in the forces and stationed in Nottinghamshire, I understood the reason for there being no change. One autumn evening, I was leaning over a lane-side gate and listening to the breeze rustling the leaves in the darkness, when several shadowy forms appeared in the field. When they were about ten yards away, I without thinking gave the poachers' call sign, and sure enough it was answered! The men came across to me and seemed surprised when they saw I was in uniform. They wanted to know where I did my poaching and I replied, "On the Welsh borders," not daring to say that I was a keeper in civilian life! The fact that they answered when I called brought home to me that the same call must have been used over a vast area and so would not be easy to change. I wonder if the same way of knowing those with the same purpose in mind is in use today anywhere – I myself have not heard it for many years.

The incidents I have related up to now all took place during the hours of darkness. This somehow gives a hint of mystery and perhaps even glamour to it, but you can believe me, for every poacher or gang of poachers caught, there were many, many nights when nothing happened, yet the keepers were there, patiently waiting. The daytime also required, and still requires, constant vigilance to keep poaching within reasonable bounds. It can easily be a case of "give them an inch and they'll take a mile". Somehow, poaching in the hard light of day seems to be more like hard-faced stealing; by comparison, poaching rabbits at night appears a kind of sport. A certain amount of ferreting was done by "day men", whose activities could be easily detected by just a passing glance at a rabbit burrow. I never knew a ferreting poacher yet who troubled to fill in the small holes made by the purse-net pegs, so a quick look usually revealed their activities.

One incident I recall involving ferreting poachers happened during rather frosty weather. These two men were busy ferreting a rabbit burrow next to the river bank in a narrow belt of trees when I caught sight of them whilst looking at my tunnel traps around the Duck Wood. At first I wasn't sure what the men were up to, only being able to see them moving about in the undergrowth, but I knew there was a rabbit burrow at that particular spot so thought it quite likely that they were after a coney or two. To get a better view I had to go part of the way across the plank over a rather deep ditch and, still not being able to get a clear view, I leaned rather heavily on the handrail. Being absorbed in what I was doing, I failed to notice that the handrail was slowly giving way, but when I did it was too late! I could not regain my balance and went with a resounding plop into the ditch, breaking an inch or so of ice in the process. I clambered out but in a few seconds was absolutely frozen. The men engaged on the rabbit burrow had of course heard the noise, so I shouted, "All right, I'm coming," and to keep the circulation going I ran across to them. I found them in the process of picking up the purse nets with several rabbits lying on the ground, so they must have been busy for some time. I quickly asked their names, picked up the rabbits and gathered a few nets. I was freezing, so without more ado set off, leaving them to await the re-appearance of the ferret. Once out of sight I threw the rabbits in a bush and at a brisk trot made my way home. Those poachers didn't actually have the laugh on me, but in my haste I had forgotten to get their addresses, so was not able to make them pay the usual pound to a hospital!

Very few pheasants were taken by poachers before the war, but since time immemorial there has always been someone who would have a go, no matter what the risk. One man, well known to us, was suspected of taking the odd bird but was never caught with one. Micky Moran was a notorious character, and a likeable rogue really. One autumn afternoon I was crossing the parkland in the company of Tom Starks when we came across Micky sitting under a huge oak. Tom knew him well and asked, "What plans are you hatching now, Mick?" The answer of course was "None." There were quite a lot of practically full-grown pheasants in the area, so Tom ordered, "Turn out your pockets, Mick." With reluctance he did so, bringing to light among other things a home-made catapult and a handful of steel ball bearings. There was also a short length of long net with a ball of twine attached – Mick had been knitting a long net for the approaching netting season. A lot of men knitted their own nets but me laddo was also taking stock of where the catchable rabbits were. We were pretty certain that the catapult was to be used to get one of the pheasants, but we had foiled Mick's intentions and gained a ball of string and a catapult.

What few birds were taken in those days appeared to go in the daytime. We never caught a pheasant poacher at night, nor one with a gun or the like capable of killing a bird. There were very few trespassers at Eaton in those days as practically every drive had a lodge at the entrance and the lodge-keeper made sure that no unsavoury or suspicious character used the drives. The 2nd Duke allowed the public to walk these drives, but they were fully aware of the privilege and it was very rare to see anyone even on the grass. Perhaps the number of keepers around helped, too.

I was with old Ted Milton one afternoon at about the time that the pheasants were beginning to leave the wood and explore the surrounding field. One particular field, the barley field, had a good crop of thistles on it and was a favourite place for the pheasants, who obviously enjoyed the insect life created by the weeds. As we got near the field we could see a man rambling about it quite close to the wood, carrying a basket and a stick. Ted said, "That devil's after mushrooms. Let's go and get him." We duly came up to this man and Ted said, "You're not allowed here, empty your basket." The chap started giving Ted some cheek, saying, "If you want mushrooms, gather them yourself." Ted, normally a placid man, reacted very quickly when riled, and with one blow from his ashplant he knocked the half-full basket from the man's hand. Fortunately I had moved round a bit and we had this chap between us, because the next second he dived at Ted with the knife he had been using to cut the mushrooms. Like a flash Ted shouted, "Hit him!" With that the man stopped in his tracks and spun round to face me, whereupon Ted lifted his stick and, giving one almighty swipe, wrapped it round the man's neck. Yes, literally wrapped it

round his neck — for a split second it looked like a stick necklace!
That was that, for when the chap had pulled himself together he
departed like the proverbial hare! Ted said "Let him go, he won't
be back again for a long while." We refilled his basket with the
spilled mushrooms and, picking up the trespasser's fallen stick, I
noticed feathers adhering to it. Ted examined these closely and
decided they were pheasant's feathers. So it wasn't only mushrooms
the trespasser had been after — he must have been hitting out at the
very tame pheasants on this particular field. That story illustrates
why anyone not entitled to be on the land in those days was always
treated as a suspicious character.

Today, with people having much more leisure time and trans-
portation being so much easier, there are a lot more trespassers
although I am afraid that a lot of the offenders do not think of it as
such. This of course makes it that much more difficult for the
gamekeepers, for anyone intending to take a pheasant or two can
easily go about in the guise of a rambler, concealing a modern air
rifle which can be a powerful weapon.

Shortly after the last war, when things began to get moving
again and pheasants were once again being reared, quite a few birds
were taken by people shooting from motor cars. Mostly a .22 rifle
would be used, a comparatively quiet weapon, and it was quite easy
for these "gentlemen" to get several pheasants in the course of an
hour or two's drive in the country. Commercial travellers were
often involved in this and, covering such a large area as they do,
were seldom caught. Now motor cars are still used in most cases of
poaching but in rather a different style. As a rule any night
poachers are now brought by car to the area in which they are
going to operate and arrangements made by them to be picked up
either at a given spot or sometimes after one of them has been to
the public phone box. Because they do not always go back to the
dropping-off point, unlike the old-time poacher who invariably
came by cycle and had to return to it, it is not very easy for keepers
to combat these methods, but keepers are no fools and have been
able to deal with the menace reasonably well. Many Game
Departments now have personal radios which enable the where-
abouts of any poaching to be monitored and plans to be laid to catch
the miscreants. The poachers are of course aware of the use of
radios, but gamekeepers have other tricks up their sleeve, which I

have no intention of disclosing! The local police in my experience have always been most helpful, and always ready to co-operate in any attempts to deal with the poaching fraternity. It is of course a big asset if the local bobby is a country man and keen on country sports; some are very fond of a shot or two, and can usually be found a chance of an afternoon's shooting.

Apart from pheasant and rabbit poaching, there are of course other goings on in the country that the efficient gamekeeper cannot afford to overlook. Take coursing. It is not unusual to see several men with dogs, mostly of the whippet type, walking across the land. For a long while I could not understand why these trespassers nearly always had a terrier or two with them but, after watching a gang operating, did in the end discover how they used these dogs. The method used by proper coursing clubs is to line out across a field, with the two dogs due to course roughly in the middle of the line. When a hare is put up, and after it has about an eighty-yard start, the greyhounds are "slipped" and from then on judged on their performance. But the poaching gangs, usually three or four in number, cannot cover enough of a field to put up the hares, so this is the job of the terriers. Terriers of all sorts are used but the Jack Russell type is the most popular – a busy, lively little dog that ranges far and wide and, having a very useful nose, will put up most of the hares on a field. These men are usually not so interested in the performance of the dogs, their object being to kill the hare, whereas a coursing club would prefer the hare to escape once the qualities of the opposing greyhounds have been judged.

Sometimes these trespassing dog men have a genuine greyhound with them, as opposed to the usual whippet-type dog, and there is evidence that these dogs are being trained for a local greyhound track. When some of these gangs have been caught, there has been amongst them one man who seems out of place and frequently comes from further afield: the owner of a greyhound being trained?

In the last ten to fifteen years this type of trespasser has increased dramatically; there are several gangs operating all over South Cheshire, and no doubt in many other places as well. Although it takes place in daylight most of the time it is not easy to waylay them as they are dropped off and then picked up at a different spot, maybe after a phone call. We have been pretty successful at Eaton and one of these "gentlemen" has been convicted almost twenty times for this offence on this Estate alone. Sometimes this coursing method of poaching takes place at night, and then the gang use one of the readily available, modern, high-powered lights. It makes it much easier for a watching keeper to know when they are about, but it is not always easier to catch them for once the light is out, they can just disappear into the darkness.

The poachers of today are much more hard-faced than their pre-war counterparts, but just as cunning in their use of diversions to try and distract the keepers' attention whilst they go about their unlawful business. Soon after motor cars began to be used as a means of transport by these men, we were night watching at Aldford some time in November. Around midnight we saw the lights of a car stop about half a mile away. Ron Jones was on duty with me that night, and of course we were a bit suspicious when this car stopped. After a while the lights came on again and in the stillness of the night we could hear an engine revving up. This went on for a while so, as everything seemed quiet, we decided to go and investigate. On arriving at the spot we found a well-dressed man of about thirty standing in the lights of the vehicle surveying the situation. One rear wheel was bogged down and, despite all his efforts, he had been unable to move the car. He told us he had been careless and had inadvertently run off the road. We gave him a push and he was soon on the hard road again. He thanked us and, as he drove off, gave a couple of toots on the horn. Of course we did not take the number of the motor, which probably wouldn't have helped much in those days anyway. As everything else seemed quiet, we spent another half-hour or so at that end of the beat before calling it a night and going home. The next day we wished we had retraced our steps for the wood we had been watching, the "Sourbutts", had been visited. To judge by the bunches of feathers on the ground, several pheasants had been taken. It was never absolutely certain, but to my mind the bogged-down car was a decoy. The gang could have got it out without much trouble if they hadn't been disturbed, and the two toots on the horn could so easily have been a warning to them.

They are cunning devils, these poachers, but as a rule most gamekeepers can keep stroke with them. Nevertheless, I feel sorry for any keeper who is single-handed: it is impossible for one man to keep watch twenty-four hours a day, so no matter what, even with the best of co-operation from the local police, there are many hours when roosting birds are wide open for the attention of human predators.

I would like to complete this chapter, mainly about poaching ancient and modern, with a little bit about something which is not actually poaching – in fact it is really a very ancient "sport" – but which now, due to an Act passed in the mid-1960s, is illegal. Badger digging or baiting was a sport of the landed gentry in the distant past, and small tough terriers such as the Jack Russell were bred specially for this purpose. In a way I suppose it was akin to fox hunting but the badger, although not at all ferocious, is a very strong animal and will put up a savage fight if cornered. It was this that made badger baiting so popular: gentlemen would back their terrier against another, much as one cock bird was backed against another in cock fighting (now also illegal). I doubt if the baiting of badgers made much difference to the population of "Brock"; there has always been a large number at Eaton and, although the number fluctuates, I can detect little change over the years. Unauthorised digging out of the badgers did increase during the early 1960s, and for a variety of reasons. Very few rabbits were about after the "myxy" outbreaks and many people feel a need to follow a country pursuit of some sort, even without permission. This contributed to the tendency to dig the badger.

In a roundabout way, the Act banning badger killing has even contributed to the activity. The type of people that break the game laws and other countryside laws often do so just for the devil of it, and soon after the badger Act was passed we had a spate of badger digging. Some of the miscreants arrived with the same dogs as were used in pursuit of hares, since the terriers used for putting up the hares could also be used in a badger sett. Indeed, the first gang caught at Eaton going after badgers was led by the man I mentioned earlier who had been convicted many times for poaching hares. This case was only the second one brought under the new Act and resulted in a pretty hefty fine. Since then another conviction has been obtained, but this time the people involved came from Manchester, some forty-five miles away. Another incident has occurred since then and an appearance in court is pending. These cases suggest that more digging of badgers is going on now than ever did before the Act made it illegal. Perhaps the new law has done some good, since at least convictions can be obtained, but even this doesn't seem to stop the barbaric activity.

8

So for my first ten years on the Eaton Estate the seasons revolved nicely and cosily, with the occasional excitement. His Grace was in residence at more or less fixed periods: the Grand National, Chester Races, a tennis week when the tennis stars of the day would be at Eaton and play with the other guests. Several weekends had golfing parties to play on the nine-hole private course, and there were the shooting parties in November, December and January. Like so much else, all this was to be changed by the Second World War.

When war broke out in September 1939 the woods at Eaton, as I suppose on most large estates, were full of half-grown pheasants. The 2nd Duke had also taken the shooting at Worlds End again, so there were a large number of birds there as well. Several of the younger keepers, the lads, had already been called up for National Service. There did not appear to be anything dramatic happening, but of course there was much apprehension about what the future would hold. Pheasant shooting provides a large amount of food, but even in those distant days it was an expensive sport. What was the saying then? "Up goes a penny, down comes a pound" — meaning the cartridge cost a penny and the pheasant that was (one hoped) falling to earth had cost twenty shillings to produce! I won't try to compare that with today's prices, but in comparison the costs are nowhere near as high, otherwise many small shoots would have gone by the board now.

Bend-Or, the 2nd Duke, was an intensely patriotic man, as was shown by his First World War record (the 4th and 5th Dukes were both badly wounded in the last war and Gerald, the present and 6th Duke, is a part-time soldier, serving in the Cheshire Yeomanry). It wasn't long after war broke out that we received orders to economise as much as possible on the pheasant feed. This is not easy to do because growing birds, being ever hungry, will trail after anyone that comes near them if they are underfed. But we had to cut down somewhat so, although the birds had very little less to eat, we cut out feed that had to be imported, such as maize. Early in October of that year Major Basil Kerr, the Estate Agent, paid one of his routine visits to see the pheasants feeding and said that he thought the Duke would want to shoot much earlier that season. It was therefore no surprise when it was announced that the shoot would be the last weekend in October, a month earlier than was normal, but none. of the keepers was very pleased because the rearing programme had been geared to a late November shoot. With the slight cutback in protein-rich food, the pheasants were not maturing as quickly as usual, so no optimism was expressed over the coming shoot. I was in a slightly better position than most of the keepers because I had taken over the Aldford beat on getting married in April 1939 and had moved to the cottage at Aldford where I still live. The beat I had taken over always had the first birds from the rearing field, but even these would be hardly mature by the end of October, although they should fly reasonably well. No matter, the Duke intended to shoot early and thus save a large amount of food: pheasants consume about ten hundredweight per hundred per week, so with a good many thousand crops to fill, the savings in a month would be considerable.

The shoot eventually took place and, as was expected, was not too big a success. The shooting at Worlds End was reasonable

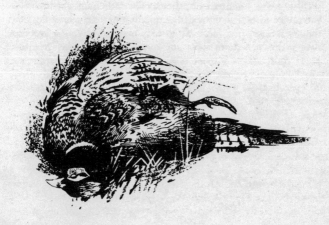

though – the pheasants there did not have much option but to fly higher, being driven off a mountainside! As His Grace was leaving the day's shooting at Aldford, after thanking everyone as usual, he turned to Sandy Myles and said, "No more shooting this season. Catch them all and make it as soon as possible." Once more he was thinking about the feed, and even the powder used in the cartridges.

It was an unusual task to have to catch so many pheasants, but after a few days to let them settle down after the disturbance of a shoot, a start had to be made. It was clear that the method used to catch pheasants for the laying pens would not be satisfactory when dealing with such large numbers, so coops were used – it was possible to catch sometimes two or even three birds in a coop at a time. The coop fell over the birds with only a dull "plop" and the pheasants, being in darkness, did not flutter, so little disturbance was caused. With about fifty coops set on a feed ride, inroads were soon made into the hundreds of birds left after the shoot. Although it was hard work, back and to along the row of coops, the most heart-breaking part was having to kill the birds when they had been caught. Eventually the task was completed, leaving rather more birds than was usual as a breeding stock, although we knew that few of the hen-birds would be successful in rearing a brood.

After the woods had been more or less cleared of pheasants, we set about the task of dealing with the rabbits. It was obvious that in time of war it was essential that the land should produce as much as possible, and a large number of rabbits don't help in that respect. I did mention earlier that Aldford was a different type of soil from Eaton Park, being more sandy, so the main weapon against the coney was the gin trap, but there were several patches of kale which yielded many hundreds of rabbits. The technique was to arrange for tracks to be cut through the middle, then set a long net down the track and drive the kale, at the same time having a keeper or two on the outside to shoot any coney trying to leave. It made a great sport and was more enjoyable than the work of trapping.

Even by the summer of 1940 there was little change in the countryside caused by the war. Quite a few estate employees had already been called up or had joined their unit, as workers had always been encouraged to join the Territorial Army, in this case the Cheshire Yeomanry. During 1940 an Observer Corps post was established at Aldford and many residents joined the Corps to man it, mostly pensioners who could put in the duty hours much more easily than an employed person could.

When the Home Guard was formed it was certain that the gamekeepers would be involved. Keepers obviously knew every inch of the area and were skilled in the use of firearms, so the very first week after the formation of the Home Guard, all keepers were issued with the armband which denoted that they were members. There was no option with Sandy Myles in charge – he just arrived with the armband and said, "You will be on duty at 8 pm. Report to the pub." At least he chose not a bad assembly point, I suppose!

The Home Guard created many amusing incidents, but behind it all was a deadly seriousness. I must admit, though, looking back on it, that in the early stages we would not have done the slightest bit of good! That summer of 1940 we were on duty from 8 pm to 6 am, three men at a time, and although it was usually arranged for one keeper to be on duty with his gun, little was achieved apart from checking late-night travellers. One night, I remember, I was on duty with two of the local farm workers. We had a hut for shelter and one man was on duty on the road whilst two rested in the hut. Although it was a lovely summer night, the temperature drops towards dawn and one man had brought an oil stove for a bit of heat. All was very quiet when I took over patrolling the road at midnight. An odd dog barked in the distance and I could hear an owl calling its young in a nearby wood. An occasional aircraft passed high overhead, but with no sign of parachutes falling. The time went on and I was quite happy, listening to the night sounds. It got to four o'clock, so I thought I would stir the next one on duty, who should have been on at two. I went to the hut, opened the door and was greeted by a cloud of smoke belching out from the old oil stove. I shouted, "Come out," but nothing happened so I had to go in, half-expecting to find my companions unconscious from the dense fumes. They both stirred, and one said, "Is it my turn?" I was so glad to hear a voice, but having helped them outside, I just had to burst into laughter – their faces in the dawn light looked as if they were members of the Black and White Minstrels! When it became fully light the inside of the hut was festooned with soot-laden cobwebs, but what a good job the men were asleep on the floor and must have been below the acrid, soot-laden smoke.

During the daytime that summer, most of the younger keepers would work on the farms helping with the hay harvest. As a large proportion of the Aldford beat is the Home Farm, I gave what help I could there. There seemed a great urgency to get the crops gathered in good order that summer, so any assistance to speed up the process was appreciated and encouraged.

Eventually my turn came to join the armed forces and at the end of July I went to my appointed unit, a light anti-aircraft regiment. After the usual initial training I was posted to a battery stationed at Leyland, Lancashire, and spent my duty hours manning a Lewis gun. These guns were mounted in what were judged to be strategic positions as the best possible defence against the low-flying bombing raids which were being carried out at that time. One such post was on the roof of Leyland Motors, and one dull, misty November day in that year of 1940, I was manning the position with another gunner. After an hour or so, my colleague decided to go to the canteen for a cup of tea – this was against regulations, but soldiers were always welcome in the canteen. Soon after he left, I heard the dull drone and throbbing of an engine to the south-west. Keeping a sharp eye in that direction, I suddenly caught a glimpse of an aircraft in the gloom. All British planes had to keep flashing a certain series of lights, which were changed each day. This craft was showing no lights at all, so I swung the Lewis gun round onto it just in case and when it was almost overhead I saw something leave the plane. Swinging the gun right round and giving the target a good lead (like a high-flying pheasant), I pulled the trigger and emptied the "pan" at it. The magazine was loaded with every fifth cartridge a tracer, so I could see where I was shooting and that the plane was catching some of the bullets. As it disappeared into the low cloud I could see flames and smoke coming from one engine of what I had by now recognised as a German Heinkel.

After duly entering the incident in the log, but omitting the absence of my colleague, I realised that the bomb the plane had dropped had failed to go off. Later, the Battery Major told us that the plane had crashed in the Pennines, and after he had visited the spot he gave me a piece of metal from the fuselage, which I have to this day.

I was eventually posted to a Brigade H.Q. where I was to become batman to the Brigadier, but soon the Brigade was mobilised for overseas and I found myself as batman to General O. T. Frith at 5th Anti-Aircraft Group H.Q. The General had picked me out for this post because he was a shooting and fishing man; in Anti-Aircraft Command one day a week was free of duties, and whenever possible the General took advantage of this and indulged in his favourite pastimes. Many places throughout the north of England I visited with the General, and although no rearing of game was taking place, quite good bags were obtained and much sport enjoyed.

I do not pretend to know a lot about fishing, but I think the General thought I did or should. Really I was lucky in this respect, for one evening he was dry-fly fishing for trout in a well-stocked lake. The fish were rising well, but no matter what fly the General put on his line or how much he thrashed the water, there was never a taker. After a number of futile attempts he turned to me and said, "Mursell, you put one on." This was something of a problem: the General was reputed to be a very good angler, and if he had tried various flies but still failed to connect, it made it difficult for me to pick one. No matter, whilst the trout had been refusing to look at any of the lures presented to them, I had observed that a minute black fly or midge was dancing about on the surface of the water. There was no evidence that the fish were feeding on this minute insect, but I thought it was a possibility so, hunting through the fly-boxes, I chose the smallest black artificial object I could find. Tying it to the line in a rather less than expert fashion I said, "Try that one, sir."

The General looked at the object on his line and all he did was grunt. He studied the water, went through the usual drill to get the right length of line going, then made a marvellous cast right over an area where a trout was rising regularly. The moment the fly hit the water the trout rose, the General struck the instant it connected, and in a short while I had the pleasure of netting a fish of between two and a half and three pounds. Now was that senior officer pleased? I'll say he was! "Well done, Norman," he said, and from that day on, whenever we were off duty, he always used my Christian name. I suppose really it was all because of the training in observation I had received during the earlier years at Eaton.

During the time I was batman to General Frith there was a combined parade of 5th AA Group personnel and a Fighter Group Headquarters in the area. Word did not get out who was to inspect the parade, but it was obviously someone important. It was not normal for batmen to go on such parades but General Frith gave me a direct order that I was to do so. The day arrived, and all personnel paraded in best battle dress with all the essential spit and polish. An R.A.F. band played and the inspecting officer appeared – Mr Winston Churchill! He walked up and down the lines of troops, attended by various senior officers, both Army and R.A.F. He passed me, but after about five yards came to a sudden halt, putting the following officers in some confusion. Turning round, he came back and addressed me: "From Eaton, Gunner?" All I could stammer in reply was "Yes, sir." He told me to stand at ease and went on to talk about the shooting days he had enjoyed, then said, "When we have dealt with this affair let's hope we shall have some more." The attending officers did not bat an eyelid, but I could tell they were amazed. After bidding me "Good luck, soldier" Mr Churchill said to an R.A.F. officer, "That man once had the audacity to put a feather in my hat." What a man, what a memory! I now realised why the General had insisted that I attended this parade: he knew Mr Churchill was coming and, as we had spoken of "Winnie's" visits to Eaton, thought it would be nice for me to be there. However, I am certain from the way he approached me that Mr Churchill was not forewarned of my presence.

Leave is always an important thing to members of the armed forces, never more so than during war time, so I always appreciated the days I could get back to Eaton and if possible spend some time with the keepers, by now reduced to a skeleton staff of older men. They had plenty to keep them fully occupied, even if it was only the ever-present menace of hordes of rabbits. On one such visit home I went to see Fred Milton, and he asked me if I would join them the next day when live rabbits had to be caught. I jumped at the chance, and the next day met them at the chosen spot. Purse nets were being used to bolt the rabbits into, and boxes were available to place the live bunnies in. I was rather curious as to why the rabbits had to be caught alive and handled so carefully. Fred told me that the Duke had introduced a new sport for his own entertainment: hunting rabbits with his small pack of dachshunds!

The Eaton gardens in those days were rabbit-proofed either by wire netting or by a water-filled sunken fence, and this was where the Duke did his hunting or coursing of rabbits with the little short-legged dogs! Only Fred was present when a rabbit was released and then a few minutes later the Duke would send his dogs off in hot pursuit. Many of the rabbits were not accounted for by the dogs, so the next day a gang had to be organised to shoot any that had escaped the dogs' attentions. The gardeners joined in, anxious that no rabbit should survive to destroy some of the precious and rare plants. Care had to be taken that this task was done at a time when any shooting would not disturb the Duke, so the valet was consulted before starting.

That dachshund pack once caused me some embarrassment. Whilst pheasant shooting during the early days when I was still carrying cartridges for Fred, His Grace brought four or five of his favourite dachshunds out with him, all with long leads attached. At the first rise I had to try and control these little dogs and of course the leads soon got well and truly tangled. But worse was to come. As soon as the first rise finished His Grace turned to me and said, "Let Dempsey go." I hadn't the slightest idea which was Dempsey, for the dogs were as like as peas in a pod, so I let one off the lead in hope. The Duke didn't say anything, but he had a smile on his

117

face and I'm sure he wanted a dog released just for the fun of it. After the next rise he told me to let a different dog off, but I had taken Fred's tip and by watching the dogs had quickly spotted the one that reacted when its name was spoken. This continued at each rise, but I was delighted when the Duke said as he left, with a broad grin on his face, "Thank you, Mursell. You only made one mistake."

One summer leave, Ron Jones (who had been on the first poacher encounter) called on me and suggested that we went to seek some mushrooms early next morning. At that time I was not particularly fond of mushrooms, but my wife was so at least she was looking forward to a feed. It was before dawn the next morning when I arrived at Ron's home, but he was already afoot so we were soon away across the fields in the search for the most edible of fungi. Within an hour or so the basket Ron had brought was almost full, so we headed for home. As we approached the back door opened and a most delicious smell of home-cured bacon being fried wafted across the breeze. Ron's wife shouted, "I hope you pair have got some, the bacon is nearly ready." Soon the aroma of cooking mushrooms mingled with the smell of bacon, and if a man wasn't hungry, he would be after a sniff of that. I really enjoyed that breakfast and in fact have been fond of mushrooms from that day to this. There were plenty of mushrooms for all, and later that day my wife enjoyed hers, but stewed this time, not fried. Today, with the treatment the fields have been getting, mushrooms are not so plentiful and the cultivated ones are but a poor shadow of the field variety.

On 12 February 1946 I returned to civilian life. That February was the wettest on record for many, many years, and on arriving at Aldford I discovered that the bridge over Aldford brook was under water. I was even told that the previous day the water had been flowing over the bridge wall, with swans passing over! Even wading through two feet of water, it was a pleasant thought that perhaps now the whole of my time would be spent on the land I loved.

Of course nothing moved very quickly in the shooting world after such a devastating war, and there were now only four keepers employed on the Estate, compared to twenty before the war. Sandy Myles had died and my old teacher, Fred Milton, had taken on the duties of Head Keeper.

His Grace gave instructions that I was to carry on where I left off, which was all right in theory, but things had changed so much during the war that it did not quite work out in practice. There was of course no pheasant rearing, and only a small stock of birds on

the Estate. I spent a year or two dealing with the still large numbers of rabbits and keeping the predators down to a reasonable level, in the hope that before long it would be possible to rear pheasants again. Rabbits were in big demand as there was still rationing of most things, and people who liked bunny were always glad to get hold of a couple. We had been killing a few one day and taken them to Fred Milton's, and whilst we were there an old lad appeared saying, "I see you've got a couple for me, Fred." I could tell Fred wasn't too pleased, but he picked out a couple for him, whereupon the chap said, "Thank you, Fred." Fred grunted in reply, "I've got two bags full in the shed round the back." The visitor brightened. "Perhaps I could have another couple then." "No, not two bags of rabbits, two bags of thank-yous," replied Fred. It appeared that this old chap was a regular caller for rabbits, and although locals were welcome to a feed, it had come to Fred's ears that this particular fellow was not averse to selling them. I gather he didn't call again!

Towards the end of the war His Grace had purchased several large estates around the country, Penrith, Guildford and large places in Norfolk and also at Ellesmere, Salop. In 1951 there was a degree of improvement in the animal feed business, and although a large variety of feeds were still rationed, it was decided that an attempt would be made to rear some pheasants for release in Norfolk on the Melton Constable estate. Preparations were made to put this project in hand, and all went well until the chicks were hatched. The food available was so different to pre-war that it was really a case of trial and error to find out what was suitable. However, we managed to rear a nice number of birds, with the right sort of weather that season making the task a little easier. In due course the poults went down to Norfolk to augment the quite considerable stock of wild birds.

There was already a staff of keepers on the Melton Constable estate so it was their responsibility to care for the pheasants and of course to provide adequate sport for the Duke when he visited for the shooting in November. Apparently when the shoot did take place His Grace was happy with neither the quality nor the quantity of birds shown, and after two shoots did not go again that season. The next year the feed situation had improved and more birds were reared for Melton. As soon as the rearing field had been cleared at Eaton, Major Kerr, the Estate Agent, decided that someone from Eaton should go to Norfolk and try to improve the quality of the shooting. It was therefore arranged that I should travel down and see what was needed. One of the agents at Eaton, Albert Mitchell, was at that time spending every week in Norfolk in charge of farm modernisation, so transport was readily available for me. Travelling by road with Albert, going down on a Monday and returning on a Friday, became my routine for a good many weeks. After my first inspection of the estate, I recommended several steps that could be taken to ensure more sporting shots, and it was decided to carry out this work under my supervision. Some of the steps to be taken did not please the agent on the estate, but the Head Keeper was in full agreement with the action being taken, so the work went ahead. Some timber had to be felled and some undergrowth cleared to make the "flushing" point further from the guns. This duly provided good, high, sporting shots, and that season the Duke had a number of good days, although of course they did not compare in numbers with pre-war shoots at Eaton.

Nineteen fifty-three was a sad year for Eaton and many other places as well. His Grace had been on a fishing trip to Norway in a chartered yacht (the *Cutty Sark* having been taken over by the Navy on the outbreak of war) and on return to his Scottish estates was taken ill and passed away. It was a great blow to all who knew and loved him and words of mine cannot express the feelings of so many who held him in high esteem, but Seton Gordon's tribute must express it so adequately. Mr Seton Gordon was a great personal friend of Bend-Or, and his words give an insight into a man of whom the world often got the wrong impression. Immensely wealthy, fond of sport and going his own pleasure-seeking way was how most people would describe the 2nd Duke of Westminster. No picture could be further from the truth. Mr Seton Gordon says:

"Bend-Or had, in a remarkable degree, the qualities of kindliness, chivalry, courtesy and consideration for others. He was a stimulating yet elusive character, difficult to portray. Indeed to his intimate friends it often seemed that he wished the world should have a wrong impression of him. He had the qualities of the traditional Highland Chief – not only on his Sutherland Estates, but at Eaton, in Cheshire and elsewhere – and was a Father to his people. In the Highlands, he spent some of the happiest hours of his life. He had a most profound and detailed knowledge of his Estate at Eaton, home of the Grosvenors for many hundreds of years, for he had the good fortune to have grown up at Saighton Grange, the Dower House of Eaton, and it was during his boyhood that he learned to know tenants and employees so well. Bend-Or was a shy man, but once one had become his friend he was loyal, constant and great-hearted, admiring and enjoying in his friends independence of thought and independence of spirit. He had a strong sense of humour, no man enjoyed a harmless joke with more zest. His insight into a man's true worth was shown in the exceptional staff who managed, and still manage his great Estates. His relation with these men was that of one friend to another, they were a happy family, each one revering their Chief, yet not hesitating to speak their minds to him, fearlessly should the occasion demand it. That personal touch is a rare thing to find these days.

"He was great-hearted, and had the rare quality of being able to forgive one who had wronged him, he harboured no resentment against any man and lived up to his strong and simple faith in the ultimate goodness which he sought for humbly throughout his three-score years and ten.

"He was most at home with simple folk. Each year at Lochmore he invited the people on his Highland Estates to a ghillies' ball at the close of the season. It was his custom to entertain the stalkers, gamekeepers and ghillies to a dram in the dining room, while the Duchess was hostess to their wives in her sitting room. This social gathering was the prelude to a Highland Ball, and all too soon the reminiscences of days on the hill were disturbed by the sound of the pipes summoning the gathering to the opening reels. One night as the last of the guests were leaving the dining room, the Duke turned to a friend and said to him with that emphasis so characteristic of him, 'If I could have these men to dine every night of year, I would be the happiest man in the world.' That happiness which had eluded him so long he found in the last years of his life, and only those who knew him intimately could sense the depth of contentment of mind which he enjoyed in those years. Before leaving Scotland for Norway a few weeks before his passing he had remarked, 'I have never been so happy in my life.' He died as he lived, brave, undaunted and untouched by illness or old age. Now he has passed over on the crest of the wave and has left behind him a happy memory that will remain always with those who knew him."

I make no apologies for quoting the foregoing extracts from Seton Gordon's tribute to Bend-Or (by kind permission of Anne,

Duchess of Westminster). It would be impossible for me, as a servant of such a great man, to describe his character so effectively.

After the passing of Bend-Or it was of course inevitable that many changes should occur at Eaton. The young pheasants were growing rapidly, and we all wondered what the position would be regarding the shooting. The heir to the Dukedom was unknown at Eaton, and in the event was never to come to Cheshire, being apparently content to remain on his property in East Anglia. As the time to shoot approached we learned that Colonel Gerald Grosvenor and his brother, Colonel Robert Grosvenor, would be organising the shooting parties. Colonel Gerald was next in line for the Dukedom and later came to live in Cheshire, whilst his brother remained in Northern Ireland on his estate there.

Around this time the decision was made to pull the Gothic Eaton Hall down. After it had been occupied by the Red Cross, Dartmouth Naval College and after the war by an Officer Cadet Training Unit, apparently dry rot had taken over to an alarming degree. So Colonel Gerald went to live at the old Dower House at Saighton and soon became a very popular figure throughout the area.

The 2nd Duke was sadly missed. Although during the war years his sporting activities had been restricted and his shooting limited to ducks and snipe, he spent most of his time at Eaton. Being intensely interested in all things rural, particularly the Home Farm (where pedigree shorthorns were bred and reared, many of them becoming champions at agricultural shows and even the Royal Show), he must have enjoyed his closer contact with his farming activities. He was a fearless man, but when "Lord Haw-Haw", the traitor who broadcast from Germany during the war, declared that Eaton Hall would be bombed, he took action. One of the larger keepers' huts was moved into the densest part of the Fox Covert and fitted out as a comfortable bedroom. Tapestries lined the wooden hut, and as far as possible all mod cons were installed; it was during the summer months so fortunately no heating was required. Each night with his valet he would drive to the wood and spend no doubt a restful night there. Eaton was never bombed, but the adjacent village at Aldford received quite a lot of attention from the enemy, with many high-explosive and incendiary bombs being dropped. Luckily only minor damage was caused.

9

Like the 2nd Duke, Colonel Gerald Grosvenor was at heart a countryman and, although it naturally took some time for him to settle down and become acquainted with the tenants and staff at Eaton, they quickly took him to their hearts. At the time of Bend-Or's death he was living in Gloucestershire, where he stayed until the Dower House at Saighton was ready for occupation. Saighton Grange, as the Dower House is called, commands a wonderful view over a large part of the Estate and also part of Chester. After the shooting season of 1953–54 there was some speculation as to whether rearing of pheasants would continue, but Colonel Gerald soon let it be known that as far as possible, it was his wish that things should continue as before. This was cheering news as most people had been rather pessimistic about the future of the Eaton Estate, half-fearing that it would be broken up in a dispersal sale as has happened to so many large estates since the war. Things could not be the same of course. In effect Colonel Gerald was the head of the Grosvenor family but all the vast properties were controlled by the executors of the 2nd Duke's will. Later the Trustees took over for the 2nd Duke, astute businessman that he was, had created a Trust for the benefit of all future Dukes. Although a sort of care-taker, Colonel Gerald took great interest in all activities on the Estate. He had no family of his own but it was really amazing how he dedicated himself, with his wife, to acquiring knowledge of the Estate. He would often stop and have long chats with the workers, particularly the older men.

He was a keen horseman and could often be seen riding around the Estate soon after the crack of dawn – the right time to exercise a horse! Bend-Or had also been an enthusiastic horseman. He had owned a number of racehorses and at one time numerous polo ponies, having taken a polo team to America soon after the First World War. Almost up to Bend-Or's death he would often gallop round the private racecourse at Aldford. He was a great cigar smoker, and on mounting his horse would always put the cigar he was smoking on a post by the mounting block. He never retrieved it at the end of his gallop, this cigar, and it was by tradition claimed by the beat keeper! Colonel Gerald smoked a pipe and although he often galloped round the racecourse, the cigar tradition was broken.

About a third of the Estate had never been used for shooting, apart from the snipe pits and one wood which was favoured by woodcock; the only shooting there was done by the keepers when driving for rabbits. It had always been treated as purely hunting country, at least since the turn of the century, and there were two retired keepers on this fairly large area whose job was to ensure that foxes were in residence when the Hunt met. This was no great problem, as with such large numbers of rabbits there were plenty of foxes everywhere. On this Saighton section, which is well wooded and rather wet, there were quite a number of artificial earths to encourage foxes to remain in the area, as well as one or two natural earths where the land was lighter and drier. These earths were essential for the vixens to rear their cubs. Many had been there for years, but they still needed a certain amount of maintenance. Usually built on the side of a main watercourse, or in a bank beside a pond, they consist of large drainpipes buried about two and a half feet in the ground and leading to a "bed", or large, brick-lined pocket, where the fox can lie warm and snug. There are always two entrances to an artificial earth and sometimes two

beds. The Cheshire Hounds hunt this part of the Estate and it was not long before Colonel Gerald could be seen hunting with this pack, and also on occasions with Sir W. W. Wynn's pack which hunted the rest of the Estate.

Gamekeepers usually have mixed feelings about hunting, but in my experience there are very few who make hounds welcome in the pheasant coverts until the bulk of the birds have been shot, as a rule after Christmas. Country areas differ widely of course, but where the woods are spaced out as opposed to being linked up, many birds can be lost by the invasion of a pack of hounds and a horde of brilliant-coated horsemen. Where woods are some distance apart, and especially if they are on the small side, pheasants can be driven from one wood to another until, not knowing where to go, they frequently leg it to pastures new. It happens so quickly with hounds that the poor birds are soon driven to unknown territory and many of them do not return. However, most keepers like the spectacle of fox hunting and, despite their qualms about the disturbance, usually have a fox waiting for the Hunt should a local meet be inevitable. After the shooting season has ended, many keepers will follow the hounds with much enthusiasm.

After a season or two Colonel Gerald Grosvenor became Joint Master of the Cheshire Hounds with Lord Leverhulme and Lord Rocksavage (now the Marquess of Cholmondeley), so hunting was now an important factor at Eaton. It was absolutely essential that when the "Cheshires" met locally there should be one or two "long tails" in the residence. The two retired keepers who had looked after the foxes' welfare in the Saighton area of the Estate (Joe Saint and Charlie Worthington) had long since gone to join their Maker, but Colonel Grosvenor thought it would be as well to have some-one to keep an eye on Reynard on a regular basis. Togo Starks, my first Head Keeper's son, was living in the lodge at the end of the Saighton drive. Being retired, he was available for this task and could combine it with his part-time mole catching. He was ideal for the job since he knew all the woods and earths intimately and would be able to do the required earth-stopping at night without any difficulty. He had always been keen on fox hunting and had been a familiar character at local meets for many years, so he was delighted when asked by Colonel Grosvenor to help in this way. Night stopping of earths is essential to ensure that the fox is lying on the surface when the hounds draw the woods, but on a wet, rough night is not the most pleasant of tasks. Still, Togo undertook it cheerfully and obviously got much enjoyment out of a good day's hunting. His transport was a battered old motor bike, vintage the year dot, but it chugged about the countryside and managed to get Togo from one place to another.

On one occasion Togo was catching moles in the grounds at Saighton Grange when Colonel Grosvenor saw him from his study

window. He called Togo in, probably to discuss some hunting matters, and as it was a cold morning produced the whisky and gave Togo a tot. The time passed and the glasses had been refilled more than once, so when Togo came to leave, he was rather flushed and a little unsteady. The Colonel, knowing that Togo had only a short distance along the drive to go home, offered him just one more to keep the cold out, but Togo replied, "No, thank 'ee, sir, my old bike won't carry any more."

I wasn't too surprised at the story, for on another occasion I had been at the Grange and the Colonel had very kindly offered me a glass of whisky. He produced a brandy glass and poured the "mountain dew" into it. Handing it to me, he enquired, "What will you have in it, Norman?" Have in it! It was full to the brim, and difficult to hold without spilling. One like that was enough for me, so I had some sympathy with Togo, but he reached his house safely.

Hunting these days is receiving a lot of attention from the anti-blood sports people, with whom I must admit I have a certain amount of sympathy. Cruelty in any form is a distressing thing and in most fox hunts is largely avoidable, although in my experience there is much less of it now than there was years ago. Some foxes when dug out have in the distant past been thrown to the hounds alive, I do not doubt, but today the Master of the Foxhounds Association is very strict about this barbaric act. Should a fox have to be dug out, it is always killed with a humane killer before being given to the hounds, and woe betide any Master of Hounds who allows it to be dealt with in any other way. Foxes do of course suffer distress when being hunted, but the actual kill is sudden and certain, and a large number are killed very quickly indeed, often not even getting out of the wood in which they have been lying. It has been alleged that hunts have encouraged the breeding of foxes purely to hunt them, even moving a litter of cubs from one area to another to ensure a "find" when hunting that area. This may have happened but, to the best of my knowledge, not in this part of Cheshire.

I often wonder if many of the anti-blood sports people really know what actually goes on in the countryside (the seal culling is a different matter, of which I have no knowledge). It was always said that foxes killed huge numbers of rabbits. I don't think they did, even though there is no doubt that many nests of young rabbits were dug out of "stops" (shallow holes, usually in the open, where the doe rabbit has the young). Before the war, when the country was alive with rabbits, there were a lot of foxes, but today there are hardly any rabbits, at least in Cheshire, and most certainly more foxes than ever before. Now with such a large number of "long tails" about, it is very obvious to the countryman, let alone the gamekeeper, that some control must be maintained and of course hunting is a contribution to this control. I would not agree that it is the most efficient way, but when a farmer is losing a lot of lambs (and foxes do take live lambs – I've seen them) any method that is going to save the lambs is welcome. Gassing the earths is in many cases the most efficient way and probably causes least suffering. "Cymag", a powder containing cyanide, is used, and once a fox gets a sniff of the gas produced it is very soon dead. You have to make sure that a fox is in the earth when using this method, but most farmers and keepers can tell by a glance at the inward tracks whether Reynard is at home.

This method does not seem so popular these days and as usual there is a reason for it. In recent years there has been a very great demand for fox skins on the continent, foxes there having been reduced so much by rabies, so a good price is being paid for a top-quality pelt – up to thirty pounds at one time. Gassing means that the foxes are often killed deep underground, not too easy to get at, so snaring has become much more popular and is of course easier to carry out. Foxes, like most animals, have their regular runs and a snare set on one of these runs soon claims a victim. Many people can set snares, but only a few can set them so that the

intended victim is killed almost instantly; it is mainly a case of experience. By the situation of the run the setter has to judge the height and even the angle at which the snare is to be set, and he must be able to tell if it is a fox using the highway or, as is often the case, a hare. Before the war, snares of the type now used for snaring foxes were not available on the market and were usually home-made. Although they were just as efficient in catching the fox, they were often broken, so an animal was roaming the countryside with an unwanted "necklace". This did no doubt cause a considerable amount of suffering, with the fox sometimes getting entangled in bushes and dying a slow death.

Digging earths out was also a very popular way many years ago. Small terriers were put in the earth and soon gave notice if Reynard was in residence. Digging down to where the dog was barking achieved the object of the operation. This was cruel to both the fox and the terrier but, before the days of gas and adequate snares, one of the few ways to deal with surplus foxes.

Digging foxes reminds me of an incident not many years ago. The Cheshire Hounds had met at Saighton and, after good hunting, moved to draw a wood called "Platts Rough". No sooner had the hounds got into the wood than they gave tongue. No fox emerged but soon the huntsman appeared to say that one was to ground in a large rabbit burrow. Wanting to kill as many foxes as possible, the Master asked the earthstopper to dig the burrow out, and arranged for a humane killer to be available should he get to the fox. The day wore on and the earthstopper had moved a lot of earth, mostly clay, and had got down to almost five feet. No sign of the fox! Late in the afternoon, one of the gentlemen out hunting returned to see what progress had been made and, on looking down on the excavations, said, "You want a J.C.B. for that." Whereupon the earthstopper promptly replied. "No thank you, sir. I don't want any decorations. I do it for love!" Who had the laugh on who!

It would be a sorry day should fox hunting be made illegal. It is part of the rural scene, giving a lot of work and a lot of pleasure to a lot of people and killing a lot of foxes with, in my considered judgement, little cruelty. Perhaps the anti-blood sports people would achieve more if they did not take such drastic action as they do on some occasions. In the end, hunting is legal, but interference in sometimes violent ways is not. Hunting people are not cruel people, and in my experience try to do things in a most humane way. The true countryman knows the ways of the countryside and will never, I am sure, abuse the privilege of his surroundings.

In the early 1950s, when country sports were once again getting going, hare coursing started up at Altcar where the blue riband of coursing, the Waterloo Cup, is competed for each year. Even before the war Eaton had always supplied fresh blood for Altcar by catching some hares for release there. Major Kerr, the Agent, and his wife were great lovers of the sport of coursing, so on various occasions we had to arrange for "trials"; that is, the men who trained the dogs for this sport would bring their charges and let them have a course with a hare. This helped to get the dog fit and increase its keenness. It was usually arranged for these trials to take place in an area where little disturbance to game would be caused, and the farmers would join us to enjoy the sport and help generally. Interest among the farming community built up and eventually, probably at Major Kerr's instigation, the Eaton Coursing Club was formed. This meant that the Game Department had to provide a large number of hares for the coursing meeting now scheduled. There were still limited areas of green crop grown – turnips, mangolds, and potatoes – which were of great help in holding "puss", as hares are often called, but it was doubtful whether there were the hares on the land to enable courses to take place to complete the planned "stakes". It was therefore arranged for some hares to be brought back from Altcar, by kind permission of Lord Sefton, and we had to go there and help catch them. It is not difficult to net hares but it is very tiring; as it is done in the daylight, the hare can see the net and has to be chased into it. This means having a lot of men in hiding at the net and, when a hare approaches, one man on either side runs out, gets behind the hare and tries to chase it into the waiting net. We made several trips to the famous coursing ground between Liverpool and Southport, each time returning with thirty or forty hares, and released these on the area proposed for the Eaton meeting. We found it best to release the hares at dusk and preferably into a wood, since a hare will often seek cover anyway when frightened. Joe Flatman, the late Head Keeper at Altcar, gave us a lot of good advice about what was required for a coursing meeting and in fact came to Eaton and made several useful suggestions on the site.

Colonel Gerald Grosvenor took a great interest in these coursing meetings, and although he never owned a dog, he was always present at a meeting and entertained his numerous friends. Major Kerr did not own a dog either, but Mrs Kerr was a great coursing fanatic and owned several top-quality greyhounds. Many of the local farmers also owned quite good animals, and in fact some of them eventually competed in the Waterloo Cup. For quite a number of years the meetings at Eaton went great guns, usually taking place in October when there was still a fair amount of ground cover and plenty of stubble for the hares to lie on, making it much easier to get the hares onto the actual coursing field. This was a field large enough to allow the slipper (the man who released the greyhounds) to give the hare the regulation eighty yards start before slipping the dogs and also large enough for the judge on horseback to have time to decide the best performance.

After a number of years of successful meetings, Major Kerr passed away and the mainstay of the club was lost. By now farming methods were changing and there was much less cover to hold the hares, but despite conditions going against good coursing the club survived another year or two. In fact during this period Mrs Kerr's dog "Jonquil", which had won the premier stake at Eaton, went on to Altcar and won the Waterloo Cup. Great celebrations were called for on this auspicious occasion and Mrs Kerr entertained a large number of people connected with the coursing at the Grosvenor Arms at Aldford, where a right royal time was had by one and all.

During this time Colonel Gerald Grosvenor was still carrying on with the pheasant shooting on a limited scale, but he was very fond of duck shooting too, so numerous trips were made around the pits in search of "quackers". He decided that a few days' partridge shooting would not come amiss, so some partridges were reared, but with many fewer holding crops than before the war the possibilities were limited. All the same, some very pleasant days were had, although the bags were never very large.

For a year or two things were pretty hectic in the Game Department, what with rearing pheasants and partridges, duck shooting and coursing meetings, but even with a reduced staff the routine jobs also had to go on. With only four keepers some of the tasks needed help from the Forestry Department, such as squirrel shooting. Colonel Grosvenor was very keen on forestry and his wife on brightening the drive up with flowering and colourful shrubs, so the grey squirrel, being very destructive to young trees and shrubs, had to be kept down. When I first came to Eaton in 1929, grey squirrels were plentiful, but mainly in the Park, very few having spread to elsewhere on the Estate. In those days there was also quite a fair number of red squirrels but most of them had been pushed out of the Park and had taken up residence mainly at Buerton, in the Saighton area. I am not certain that greys kill the reds but they certainly do not exist together and of course the grey ones certainly do eat flesh – in fact they will eat almost anything. "Tree rats" is quite a common name for them, and seems to be a pretty accurate description of these destructive little animals. Many years ago the keepers had instructions from the 2nd Duke to kill and skin a large number of grey squirrels, enough in fact to make a fur coat for the Duchess. I don't know if it was ever made but I think somewhere around eight hundred skins had to be obtained, a pretty hefty task even in those days. I wonder if it was a long or a short coat?

During the war years the control of the squirrel population had been rather neglected, since cartridges were in short supply and in those days shooting was the main way to deal with the grey pest. At the end of hostilities, with the vast increase in squirrels and the forestry plans for large-scale planting, the Wartime Agricultural Committee (War Ag.) was offering two shillings for each squirrel tail produced. This soon brought a flood of tails, and it wasn't long before the sheme had to be dropped because of the amount of money involved.

At Eaton several forays were made after the squirrel. To start with we walked each wood and shot any squirrels we came across, but even after expending a lot of cartridges by shooting into the dreys, it did not turn out to be a very successful operation. The dreys, often built by the squirrels at a great height and made of leaves and twigs, resisted a charge of shot and very few squirrels left this safe haven. We were never sure if any had been killed in the dreys. Mr W. A. Redfern, who on Major Kerr's death had taken over as Estate Agent, arranged for the county pest officers to come with their sectional poles and demonstrate the method of poking the dreys out, thus making the squirrel leave home and present a chance of a shot. This was a great success and we were able to kill about four times as many squirrels in a day. Mr Redfern then ordered a set of poles so that we could do the job properly, but this posed a problem as it really needed three or four guns round a tree when a drey was being poked out and two men on the poles, so the Forestry Department was called upon to provide some assistance. It could be quite hard work joining the poles up and pushing them through the boughs to a drey high up in the tree-top; it would not have been so bad if there was a squirrel in residence each time, but very often it was a blank. Not too good for the morale if you came across a number like this, but it was necessary to push every drey out just in case a squirrel was at home.

The weather could make quite a difference when after squirrels. On a bright sunny day they would be out foraging and just made themselves scarce, disappearing into the tree-tops where they are most difficult to spot. Often the glimpse of a bushy tail waving in the breeze was all that could be seen — not much use shooting at that! March is about the best month to poke the dreys out and then a fair number of squirrels can be killed, sometimes two or three to a good drey. Eleven is the most I have ever seen come out of one drey. It was right at the end of the wood on a bright day, so they had obviously gone up the wood in front of us and taken refuge in almost the last drey we found. What fun that was, squirrels going in all directions and guns going off in rapid succession, sometimes, no doubt, two keepers shooting at the same target. We accounted for ten, the other one disappearing into an old woodpecker's nest!

Believe me, these little grey animals are not easy targets, jumping from swaying bough to swaying bough, and they are not very big anyway. Other methods used to control the grey are rather time-consuming, such as a wire trap which will catch a certain number but has to be visited several times a day, or tunnel traps which will pick up a few. Really, poking the dreys out is the most productive. At one time we were getting about fifty a day by this method and, on one day not many years ago, the young Earl Grosvenor as he was then (now the 6th Duke) was with the keepers and over one hundred were killed. We picked the area where most squirrels were that day! Now the grey squirrel is reasonably under control, but given a chance will soon build up to large numbers again, so the annual round-up will have to continue. The red squirrel has gone, gone for ever I should imagine, at least from this area. The last one I saw was on the bridge crossing the Aldford to Chester road in 1951.

Varied tasks come the keeper's way, from patrolling the grounds at Eaton when a ball was in progress in the old days, through rearing various types of game, ornamental wildfowl and peacocks (for the now Sally, Duchess of Westminster) to controlling pigeons, squirrels, rabbits and even moving a huge starling roost to pastures new! About 1955 many thousands of starlings took to roosting in the Fox Covert, and these birds when gathered in huge numbers can do a vast amount of damage even to mature trees. Many years earlier, when part of the Fox Covert had been a young wood, these hordes of chattering, whistling birds had spent several weeks roosting there and had killed a large number of young trees by the density of their droppings. So many trees had been either killed or spoilt that no thinning by the woodman was needed, so Colonel Grosvenor was very concerned when they re-visited the wood after so many years. On the earlier visit Dick Starks (it was that far back) had organised teams of guns to shoot into the vast clouds of birds as they came in to roost. Up to five hundred shots were fired into the invaders every night for quite a few nights. I spent a night or two there on that occasion, and although each shot cut a swathe through the low-flying birds as they approached, there wasn't even a check in the vast cloud despite numerous dead birds falling to the ground. After several thousand cartridges had been expended in this way, Dick decided it was a futile operation and gave the starlings best, leaving them literally to take over the wood until about early March when they dispersed to get on with their breeding.

Colonel Grosvenor discussed with me the possibility of moving the new wave of invaders in the 1950s and I explained the failure of Dick Starks' attempts so many years before. I don't think he was really convinced that it was almost impossible to move them once they had settled in, and he asked me to fire a few shots at them for an evening or two. I knew this was useless but carried out his request, achieving, as I had anticipated, nothing. The Colonel paid several visits at eventide – I think to make sure I was letting off a shot or two – so he could see that the starlings just ignored anything I did. Fortunately the birds did not arrive until shortly after Christmas, so the damage was not as great as if they had arrived in the autumn as they had done before.

Colonel Grosvenor was still not convinced that it was practically impossible to move them, and said he would get in touch with the county pest officers. After a week or two the chief pest officer came to see me, and we watched the huge clouds of birds coming in to roost – millions of them. He said, "I think we can deal with this problem all right" and went on to tell me that he would bring his lads with rockets and thunderflashes one evening. The days passed and no sign of the pest officers, so I asked the Colonel when they would be coming. "They tell me they are rather busy but will arrive in due course," he answered. They did come, but not until the last few days in February. Numerous very large rockets were let off, exploding in the air above the starlings as they came in to roost, but were completely ignored by the birds. When they settled in the trees, thunderflashes were exploded under the roosting birds but all they did was to rise in the sky in a huge cloud and then drop back into the wood at once. After several nights of this treatment the starlings tended to settle in the trees in the surrounding fields, but when it was almost dark they would descend like an avalanche into the wood.

A week or so later the numbers roosting gradually got less and less and eventually the unwelcome visitors dispersed completely. Colonel Grosvenor was fine and pleased and praised the efforts of the pest officers, saying, "I knew it was possible to put those accursed birds on the move." I didn't enlighten him – it was now March and "those accursed birds" were once again off to their nesting site. But I did wonder if the pest officers had really been too busy to visit us earlier, or did they know full well that come March the starlings would leave the roost anyway?

It is a marvellous sight to see those huge clouds of starlings coming in to roost, wheeling, climbing and diving almost as if one bird gives the command and the rest follow. That won't be the case, but I know of no explanation for such controlled movement of such large numbers of birds. Flocks of waders show similar control as they skim over the water.

It is amazing how the droppings mount up under a starling roost, and all the boughs and twigs on the trees become thickly coated with them; in fact, if a large roost starts early in the autumn, the boughs will become so slippery that the birds leave for another location. I wonder at the weight of so many birds on one bough, and sometimes it becomes so great that quite thick branches break under the strain. Walking through the Fox Covert one evening

with a local naturalist called Alec Taylor, who was of course interested in the starling roost, I clapped my hands and a multitude of birds took to the air. It was quite an experience to feel the heat driven down upon us by the upward movement of the birds. Alec likened it to opening an oven door, and I think that is just about as good a description as it is possible to give.

I noticed something else when the Fox Covert was used as a starling roost. On my way to inspect the artificial fox earth one day, I had to go almost to the centre of the wood. Picking my way as well as I could through the starling droppings, which were at least five inches deep, I noticed several elastic bands but for a while did not take a lot of notice. Returning from the earth I saw more of these bands, both large and small, wide and narrow, which aroused my interest. It eventually dawned on me that the starlings must be bringing the elastic bands to the wood. There could be no doubt that the birds were passing the bands through them, more than likely having picked them up in mistake for worms or something similar. Some time later, when the starlings had left and heavy rain had washed most of the droppings away, the ground was literally covered with thousands of multi-coloured bands of all sizes, and even numerous bands of the type used to seal the ordinary one-pound jam jar! I have discussed this with many knowledgeable people over the years and have yet to hear of anything similar under a starling roost. I can only assume that the voracious flocks of starlings had been spending a lot of time feeding on a Council refuse tip or somewhere similar. Where else could they have got so many elastic bands? Fortunately the Fox Covert has been free of a starling visitation since then, so I have not been able to check.

In 1961, Fred Milton, who did not drive a car and found getting round the Estate more and more difficult, decided to retire and I was honoured when Colonel Gerald's choice for Head Keeper fell on me, the climax of thirty-two years' service to his family.

10

In February 1963 the 3rd Duke of Westminster, who to the best of my knowledge never visited Eaton, passed away and was buried at the family church in Eccleston, a village on the Estate halfway between the Hall and Chester. Colonel Gerald Grosvenor now became the 4th Duke, with his brother, Lord Robert Grosvenor, next in line for the Dukedom. On inheriting the title, "Gerald Duke", as he was affectionately called, had to spend more time away from the Eaton Estate, no doubt going about the affairs of Grosvenor Estates, but he loved to get back to Eaton and ride the country lanes and byways on his hunter. A great friend to all and sundry, there was nothing he liked better than a chat to anyone following a rural pursuit and for several seasons would come almost every morning to the incubator room during the rearing period. The keepers, having had an early breakfast, made a practice of brewing a cup of tea at 10 am each morning, and the Duke often arrived when the tea had just been made.

On one of the Duke's first visits he asked if we could spare a cup for him. Of course that was no problem, so he sat on the bench and it was obvious that he really enjoyed the tea. The keepers normally took it in turn to bring fresh milk each morning but one particular day, Ian Davies had forgotten it was his turn so was despatched to the village store to get a tin of evaporated milk. Tommy Green, whose turn it was to make the tea that day, hoped that the Duke would not put in an appearance, not liking the idea of offering him tea with tinned milk instead of fresh, but of course the Duke did appear. Tea was just made so Tommy had no option but to offer a cup, and explained the situation about the milk. There was no hesitation – His Grace said, "Pour me one out, Tommy. A cup of tea will be very welcome." Sitting on the bench, the Duke drank the tea and to Tommy's surprise asked for another cup, saying, "I haven't tasted a cup of tea like that since being in the desert during the war. I've really enjoyed it." On his next visit he asked if there was any tinned milk left!

For a number of years we had been rearing a few pheasants for the estate at Ellesmere, Salop, of which Lady Mary Grosvenor had the shooting. Lady Mary, daughter of Bend-Or, the 2nd Duke, had been living at Churton for a number of years and was often to be seen exercising her labradors on the Estate. Very much like her father in a lot of ways, Lady Mary was always well liked and respected, and the tenants on the Ellesmere estate thought the world of her. Unfortunately the estate has now been sold, but I have a lot of memories of visits there. Eaton supplied a number of poults for release in the woods and Gordon Young, the keeper there, reared further birds, enough to make for a number of good shooting days.

Ellesmere estate is completely different from Eaton: the woods are large, up to two hundred acres, and all more or less joined to one another by belts of trees or rough ground. Eaton on the other hand has a fair acreage of woodland but the woods are up to a quarter of a mile apart. With the woods all being linked it is much easier to hold the birds on the shoot, but sometimes they are not quite where you want them. You obviously want them in the woods where they will provide the best sport but Gordon did a wonderful job in this respect and only on a few occasions did the best woods hold less than was hoped for.

A couple of keepers from Eaton made the twenty-mile journey to Ellesmere for most of the shoots there, and these trips were most enjoyable despite being a busman's holiday. The Eaton keepers mostly helped with the picking up, but sometimes used their dogs to flush the birds where the ground cover was thick. In the first few years that Lady Mary had the shoot, several recently planted woods had a dense undergrowth, mostly brambles, and these woods were not very popular with the beaters! The dogs were most useful in this respect, but as the years passed the brambles were smothered by the growing trees and driving became much easier. Ellesmere is a marvellous shoot; being rather hilly terrain, it is possible to provide good, high pheasants without the guns having to move too far.

Lady Mary, like all the Grosvenor family, was very kind, and she would invite the keepers from Eaton and the interested farmers at Ellesmere to a day's shooting at the end of the season. At the last shoot of the season only cock pheasants were killed and a lot of formality was dropped, so this was always a memorable day. The birds always fly fast at the end of the season, and frequently higher than usual, making really testing targets for, I must admit, inexperienced shots – at least inexperienced at high-flying pheasants! It was great sport with, as you might expect, a lot of leg-pulling and general bonhomie. Gordon Young, happy and relaxed now the season was coming to an end, always had joking remarks to pass about the farmers' and keepers' skill, like, "I'll put that gun in a vice at lunchtime" (to straighten the barrels). Or, "Why didn't you bring a walking stick?"; or "Are you sure there are some pellets in those cartridges?" It was all good fun and taken in the spirit it was meant. On one occasion, and I wouldn't like to say Gordon was responsible, one farmer, a jovial character, took a shot at a nice high pheasant at the first rise after lunch and a great shower of confetti filled the air! Someone had popped a "treated" cartridge into his pocket at lunchtime and, when challenged, Gordon said, "You wouldn't kill many less if they were all like that!"

Lunch was a very relaxed and leisurely break from the day's sport. Lady Mary was an excellent hostess and made everyone feel completely at ease, so the meal, brought down from Churton, was thoroughly enjoyed by one and all. At the end of the day there was a cup of very welcome tea and a piece of lovely fruit cake for the guns in the farmhouse where lunch had been taken, while the beaters got a tot of whisky to close the season.

Lord Robert Grosvenor, later the 5th Duke, visited Eaton often from his estate in Ireland and was always present at the main shoots, and on a number of occasions he was shooting at Ellesmere. He enjoyed his shooting, but I got the impression that he was not so keen as his brother, Duke Gerald. Nevertheless, on his Irish estate a number of pheasants were reared and some quite good shooting days were enjoyed. I made several trips over to Ireland when the 4th Duke was shooting there. At that time Grosvenor Estates had an amphibious plane, a Grumman Goose based at nearby Hawarden Airport, and this plane was ideal for landing on the loch in Ireland and of course on Loch Laxford on the Scottish estate. It was a pleasant journey to Ely Lodge, Inniskillen, normally taking just under two hours, but on my second trip things became a bit hazardous. Leaving Hawarden with ten-tenths low cloud but with a good report for the Inniskillen area wasn't too bad, but crossing the Irish Sea, the plane started to ice up and we had to lose height until free of ice. The pilot was flying on instruments with not a sight of land or sea, but he eventually announced that we were over the loch at Ely and would have to come down very low to get a landmark. The loch is dotted with numerous islands, three hundred and sixty-five I believe, so it was absolutely essential to know exactly where you were. After we had made one or two low passes over the loch, a gap in the clouds showed an island, but the pilot did not recognise it. He did eventually spot a tall tree which gave him his bearings. Coming out of low clouds and suddenly hearing the rush of water on the hull of the plane was at first frightening, but then a feeling of relief came over us — we were down! That pilot was good!

On other trips in the Goose it was exhilarating to approach Ireland from the sea and to watch the varied colours of the landscape coming rapidly closer. There seemed to be vast areas of water with the land between divided up into pocket handkerchief-size fields, on which dots could be seen moving slowly about. Those dots must have been sheep, grazing on the lush pastures. The white-washed houses stood out in the sunlight with just discernible wisps of smoke curling up from their chimneys, a rural scene if ever there was one, and I felt privileged to have a bird's eye view of it. It crossed my mind that there was the view enjoyed by high-flying birds like geese and ducks, and no wonder they could so easily pick out the secluded spots to land.

Ely Lodge is on an island and normally approached over a

bridge, but arriving by plane was different. With plenty of water in the loch the Goose taxied up a ramp onto dry land, but at low water the passengers were brought ashore by boat to within a few hundred yards of the house itself. Lord Robert's keeper, Wesley Scott, always made me welcome on my visits and we had some most enjoyable times, the Irish hospitality being almost too much occasionally!

One evening, after a hearty meal, Wesley told me he had arranged to meet some friends at a local hostelry that evening. After I had spent some time in the bar with Wesley's friends, the landlord came to me and said, "There's a customer in the other bar who would like to meet you." Wesley called, "Send him through here," and in came a veterinary surgeon who at some time during his career had spent a lot of time in the Chester area and knew many of the farmers that I knew. As the evening wore on the vet got gradually the worse for wear until at last Wesley said, "I know where he lives. We had better take him home." That was all right but, after loading the vet into the back of his own car, Wesley jumped into the driving seat and said casually, "Follow me." I didn't even know where Wesley's car was, let alone where the vet lived, but with the vet sprawled in the back seat Wesley drove off into the darkness. I stood rather nonplussed as the rear lights disappeared down the lane, but noted which way the car was heading. On finding Wesley's vehicle, I started off in the general direction that the vet's car had gone and after several miles could see some red lights in the distance. They soon disappeared but I kept on, travelling at a fair rate of knots over unfamiliar roads. There – the red lights seemed to have stopped, and wasn't I relieved to come up with Wesley at a crossroads! He said, "Thought I'd better wait in case you got lost." Apart from the occasional glimpse of a red light, I had been lost! It was a good job we seemed to be the only traffic on the roads that night.

I told Wesley to take his time and keep me in his mirror and we moved off again, arriving after what seemed ages at the vet's home. He was a well-built man and it was something of a struggle to get him into the house, but when we did, his wife appeared and insisted that we have something to eat! It had gone midnight but no matter, we had to wait while of all things she made a pan of chips – the last thing I wanted. Eventually, after something of a struggle to eat the repast, we left to return to Ely Lodge, which Wesley told me was about eighteen miles away. I noticed that the petrol gauge registered nil and thought it might be out of order, but told Wesley there didn't seem much fuel left. He replied, "No, there won't be a lot," but didn't seem the slightest bit perturbed. About three miles up the road a lane branched of and Wesley turned up this, bumping and bouncing over the uneven surface. I gasped, "Where are you going, Wesley?" to which he answered, "I think there's a wee farm up here." Sure enough there was, and on arriving in the farmyard Wesley pom-pommed on the horn. A head appeared at a window and, on asking about petrol, Wesley was told that there was a full can in a nearby shed. The bedroom window banged shut, Wesley put the petrol in the tank and away we went. I never did know if that petrol was paid for or replaced, but Wesley swore he didn't know the occupier of that rather remote farm!

It was whilst loading for the 4th Duke at a shoot in Ireland that I had to think rather quickly. In that particular area of the "green country" the foxes are always shot on sight, and in fact great efforts are made to destroy any that appear. This particular day a wood was being driven, the pheasants were coming over nice and steady and the Duke was dealing with them in the proper manner, when towards the end of the drive a cry of "A fox" could be heard. I could see Reynard dodging about in the bushes but didn't point it out to the Duke as he was still busy shooting pheasants, but soon "Charlie" broke cover and made straight for where the Duke was standing. I shouted, "Woodcock left!" and of course he swung round and looked in that direction. As there was no woodcock, he said, "What's the idea? Two more pheasants have gone over." "Yes," I replied, "and that fox has got away." It then dawned on the Duke the reason for my drawing his attention to a non-existent woodcock: he was at that time Master of Foxhounds and daren't shoot a fox no matter where he was, but at the same time, in that particular part of the world, he would not have been too popular with the locals had he deliberately let it go. A face-saving ghost woodcock!

I did not see many large bags of pheasants in Ireland, two or three hundred being a very good day, but I certainly enjoyed the hospitality and the humour of the people, despite the several wet days that were my lot on my visits.

There was an increase in the amount of shooting at Eaton from 1960 onwards and an all-round improvement in the quality of the guns. Many well-known people appeared on the list of guns, and most of them were by post-war standards very good shots: Lord Brookborough, the Duke of Abercorn and Sir Randall Baker-Wilbraham, for example. Although so many things have changed, it was and is the ability of the people shooting that makes the bag at the end of the day, and although I am not in total agreement with it, the number of birds killed is often taken as the measure of the

day's sport. Many shoots can provide a large bag with only second-rate guns shooting – second-rate, I hasten to add, as regards their skill with a gun! Given good, high birds with those guns, the bag would be considerably less, but I would take a bet that the party would have enjoyed the day much more. In my opinion it is the quality (high, fast and swerving) of the birds that counts, and Lord Leverhulme once said to me, "One of these 'tall' birds is worth a dozen on the end of the gun, and if I get a right-and-left my day is made." No doubt there on what constitutes a good day's sport.

Amongst the guests around this time were of course Lord Leverhulme and Lord Rocksavage (now the Marquess of Cholmondeley), who were Joint Masters of the Cheshire Hounds with the Duke. They always enjoyed the day's sport and were enthralled if a fox should break cover. I have seen them stand and watch the "long tail" leaving pheasants to go over their heads without even a glance! Once or twice they pointed out, after seeing a fox or two during the day, that foxes and pheasants can live together, knowing no doubt that most keepers would much rather be without Reynard. Sir Watkin Williams-Wynn, who was also a frequent visitor in those days for both partridge and pheasant shooting, was Master of the pack of hounds which took his name and was interested to see a fox or two. Sir Randall Baker-Wilbraham was a regular guest, one of the old school and a stickler for the etiquette of the shooting field. On one visit to his estate near Sandbach, Cheshire, I vividly remember his giving the guns a detailed list of do's and don'ts, and all experienced shooting men at that! But the day's sport went like clockwork, and only good can come from reminding the people concerned of the proper way to do things.

All these gentlemen were good shots, but one of this era sticks out in my mind. We were honoured by the visit of Princess Alexandra and the Hon. Angus Ogilvy. No special arrangements were made, but of course there was just a shade of difference in the attitudes to the day's shooting. Mr Ogilvy turned out to be an excellent shot and could deal very happily with the highest of birds we put over him but what really caught my eye was his style, which was very reminiscent of the pre-war gentlemen. His gun handling was excellent, and his loader told me that every movement was so controlled and easy to anticipate that it made his task simple. A grand shot, and one of the best post-war, at one stand I know he killed fifty-seven high pheasants and only had a few over fifty shots.

The twenty-eighth of February 1969 was a sad day at Eaton. Gerald, the 4th Duke, passed away after many years of suffering. He was always a cheerful man and, even when in great pain, could laugh at any humorous incident and would always enquire about people's health. After an operation in London he returned to his beloved Saighton Grange but had to take to his bed. The funeral at the family church at Eccleston was preceded by a forty-eight hour vigil by many of the Estate workers, four at a time standing for an hour around the coffin containing the last remains of the great Duke and one of the country's greatest gentlemen. The service was a memorable occasion, with the trumpets of his old regiment and a church crowded with the notability from the whole country. The village hall was full of friends, tenants and employees to listen to the relayed service. I had the honour of being a bearer at this most touching ceremony.

Life at Eaton still had to go on and now we had a new Duke, well known to us because he had spent so much time here with his brother. Lord Robert became the 5th Duke and his son, Gerald, Earl Grosvenor. Changes will always take place at times like this, and the new Duke, although being keen on shooting, decided to reduce the number of pheasants reared; as he told me, "Just tick over until Lord Gerald is old enough to run the shooting." (Earl Grosvenor was then about seventeen.) With his estate in Ireland where shooting was available, and his greater responsibilities as head of the Grosvenor Estates, he could not find time for much shooting at Eaton. For a year or two less pheasants were reared but still quite good shoots took place, and of course the young Earl was present and by now starting to learn to shoot driven birds. It was

most gratifying to see the Grosvenor heir so keen on shooting — keen he was in those days, and still is!

More or less the same guns were present as in previous years, but with several fresh faces appearing from time to time. The Duke of Abercorn, Lord Hamilton and Major Hamilton Stubber came over from Ireland and Mr Randall Sparrow, a school chum of Earl Grosvenor, also took part in the shooting. Many days were spent going round the pits and driving various clumps and spinneys with the zealous young Earl, but in a way this was not a good thing as pheasants getting up and out of thick cover, or ducks getting up from an open pit, do not present a very difficult target. But even if it was not a particularly good thing for his shooting, it gave the Earl a much better idea of the size of Eaton Estate. We of course pointed out the boundaries to him, told him the names of the farms and the farmers, and generally gave him an insight of this patch of Cheshire.

Not only with the sporting activities were things changing. I have mentioned earlier that Eaton Hall, with the exception of the Clock Tower, chapel and courtyard, had been demolished, and now a "ranch house" was built near the stable block and, for entertaining large numbers of guests, one row of stables was converted into a "long room". The ranch house is a very attractive building in the Canadian style and placed in an unobtrusive spot with an excellent view of the gardens; the long room is on one side of the courtyard and used extensively for various functions, many of them to raise money for local and national charities. The 5th Duke lived in this Canadian house when at Eaton and entertained his guests there.

In November 1970 Eaton was honoured by the presence of H.R.H. Prince Charles at a shoot. We had been aware for some time that someone special was coming to the first shoot of the season, but it was only a few days before that we knew who the guest was. The pheasants had not strayed too badly that year so we were hopeful of putting up a good show, but when the day dawned it did not look so good – it was pouring with rain, blowing hard and generally miserable. We had had a number of wet days previously and everywhere was waterlogged, with vast areas of flooded meadows, so the conditions were far from ideal.

The shooting was due to start a little later than normal as His Royal Highness had to fly down from London, where he had held his twenty-first birthday party the previous night, so we hoped the weather would clear. No such luck – as Prince Charles arrived the heavens opened, and the weather was probably bad enough to cause a postponement had he not been present. No matter, shooting started with the first drive out of kale (now Crow Wood) and to my amazement the pheasants flew perfectly. They came high, fast and nearly all of them over the guns, and nearly two hundred birds were killed in this first stand. Pheasants are normally loth to get up when it is wet, but although they were in kale, the wettest possible place, it was a great rise and a good start to the day. I don't remember the bag for the day, but I do remember that the rain hardly let up and that in fact was the wettest day's shooting I ever remember in fifty years! On later visits Prince Charles has had better luck with the weather but the pheasants have not flown any better. I was impressed with the Prince's shooting; he handled a gun absolutely correctly and shot as well as the pre-war guests, so he must be one of the top shots in the country today. His style was so much like the Hon. Angus Ogilvy that I wondered if they had been to the same shooting school.

The Duke began to suffer more and more with his health around this time and was spending longer spells on his Irish estate where the air seemed to suit him, so gradually Earl Grosvenor took over more duties at Eaton. Soon we were rearing a few more pheasants and the order of things started to change. Younger guns were coming to the shoots and for a while it was a matter of as big a bag as possible, with less emphasis on the quality. This made the young Earl rather erratic in his shooting, a problem which he has now overcome, but the young gentlemen all enjoyed themselves and that was the main thing. There was a period when the etiquette on a shooting day was not of the highest standards as far as the younger generation was concerned, but this was probably due to the exuberance of youth and there is now a great improvement in that respect. Probably things will never return to the standards of pre-war, but I trust that we shall always have the right attitude to what can so easily be a dangerous sport. Looking back, it is surprising how many changes have taken place in the shooting field, some I'm afraid I don't approve of, but there is certainly a much more friendly approach to things today, and I suppose the guns do get a lot of pleasure out of working their own dogs – that never happened pre-war!

Many of the younger generation of guns are following in their father's footsteps. The Duke of Roxburgh is a frequent visitor, and I remember his grandfather shooting at Eaton half a century ago, while the Duke of Abercorn has also followed his father to Eaton shooting, but of course some guests are comparatively new. Lord Lichfield married Lady Leonora Grosvenor and so shoots at Eaton several times a year. He is an outstanding figure at a shoot, always wearing an Australian bush hat and always seeing an amusing side to any small incident, but capable of dealing with the best of high pheasants. Lord Astor is another young gentleman seen at Eaton at least once a year. Most of the younger generation I have seen in the latter half of the 1970s have improved tremendously and are now quite good at dealing with high pheasants.

Soon after the 5th Duke's second daughter, Lady Jane Grosvenor, married the young Duke of Roxburgh, His Grace finally retired to Ely Lodge, his Irish estate, and Earl Grosvenor took over many more responsibilities, but he still managed to find time for his shooting. As he was very fond of pottering around the pits and hunting small woods out with his dogs, it was sometimes difficult to know whether it was someone poaching or not. A shot or two would be heard in one area and shortly afterwards shots maybe a mile away. It is so easy to cover the ground in a Range Rover! We soon got used to this pattern and I must admit that at times I was glad he didn't want us with him as age cannot always keep up with youth.

Everyone at Eaton was delighted when Earl Grosvenor announced that he would be married in the autumn of 1978, as there had been much speculation about this hoped-for event. His wife-to-be had been seen at Eaton on several occasions and Miss Natalie Phillips was soon to become the Countess Grosvenor. The wedding took place at Luton on 7 October and a number of employees from Eaton were invited to the reception at Luton Hoo. My wife and I were honoured to be there and a glittering event it turned out to be. Many great people and personalities were present, and I particularly enjoyed a long chat with the late Lord Louis Mountbatten, in the course of which we covered a number of topics from shooting to yachting (when he knew of my origins). Why should such a great man come to such an end? Unfortunately the wedding was marred by the fact that the Earl's father was not able to be present, having been taken ill the day before, and although he recovered and was able to visit Eaton on several occasions, it was obvious that his health was deteriorating. I was talking to him on one visit, and he said on parting, "Good-bye, old chap. Thank you for everything." I was rather touched, and left with the impression that he knew the time was drawing near. The 5th Duke passed away early in 1979, and so once again Eaton Estate had lost a great man so well beloved by all. By some twist of fate one of my old faithful retrievers died of a heart attack on the same, sad day.

Now Earl Grosvenor became the 6th Duke and his lovely wife the Duchess, and this made my service at Eaton span almost fifty years and four Dukes. His Grace now spends more time at Eaton and is often seen moving around the Estate. The passing of the 5th Duke did not make many changes as he had spent so much time in latter years in Ireland; he had little to do with the running of Eaton, but the new Duke is fully aware of his responsibilities and shows the same concern for the future of the Estate as all the Grosvenors have done.

I had reached the point when the end of my service was in sight, and expressed a wish to retire on reaching retiring age. The present Duke, thoughtful as he is, arranged matters so that it was possible for me to spend the last few months as a running-down period. I much appreciated this, realising that after working seven days a week for almost fifty years, it would be a drastic change to have literally nothing to do. Local affairs have always interested me, and when a Parish Council was first elected at Aldford I was amongst the members. It has given me a lot of pleasure from that first council meeting way back in 1950 and, after being chairman for a number of years, I still find plenty of interest as the present vice-chairman. It would be possible to put a lot on paper about the activities in a village like Aldford, where the communal spirit is so good, and which is a symbol of country life on an Estate like Eaton, but this has been about my life as a gamekeeper. Still, I offer no apologies for mentioning the help that other interests are on retirement.

Twenty-one years as a special constable have also been of great interest, and of course a great help in my profession. It is essential for a gamekeeper to have a special relationship with the local police officers. We have always been very fortunate at Eaton, and almost since I can remember, the policemen covering the vast Estate have been from a rural background and therefore aware of conditions in the countryside. Quite a few alarming incidents and some humorous ones have taken place over the years, but the presence of the local bobby has always resolved them. I owe the police a debt of gratitude. By the same standards it must not be forgotten that a gamekeeper, out and about at all hours as he has to be, can be of assistance to the police at times, a fact which most rural policemen appreciate. Even now, Dave Maddox, the beat bobby, calls occasionally for a cup of tea and to see if the "Old Crow" knows anything.

The "Old Crow"! That's a nickname I somehow acquired over the years. There are many versions of it but I think it was because of my habit of saying "Arrrh" if I wanted to comment on something or saw something I didn't approve of!

There have been and are many friends and even colleagues who have not been mentioned in these pages. They must forgive me, but their company has always been appreciated: Tom Broster, Arthur Riding, Alec Minshull, Sam Emptage, Cliff Halsall and Tommy Green, to mention but a few, some still with us, some now with their Maker, but all great countrymen.

Sam Emptage, one-time chairman of the Dee Wildfowlers' Association, was a great help when greylag geese were first introduced at Eaton. The late Tom Broster, always in charge of the game cart on a day's shoot, was a source of humour when he worked out the day's bag "on my computer" – a Woodbine packet! Alec Minshull, "the man who bends them straight", a panel-beater by trade, now a loader but one-time assistant on the game cart. He once brought me a badly-eaten pheasant he had picked up at a shoot and remarked, "Someone has a hard-mouthed dog." I examined it and, finding it was stone cold, remarked, "That's not one of today's." He has never forgotten that. It was so simple to me, but not so obvious to Alec! Tommy Green, one-time keeper, now senior Security Officer in Eaton Park, when with the Game Department once accidentally knocked my pipe into a bucket full of hot water in which there was a fair amount of washing soda. After fishing it out he remarked, "That will sweeten your smokestick up!" but not a word of apology! Grand chaps, all of them.

My days as a keeper came to an end in September 1979, a few days short of fifty years on the job. In July of that year I was honoured to receive the Country Landowners Association medal for long service, from the hands of H.R.H. Prince Charles at the Game Fair at Bowood, Wiltshire. His Royal Highness recognised me, and remembered the wet day's shooting at Eaton after his twenty-first birthday celebrations. I had previously received the

Queen's Jubilee Medal in 1977 for an undisclosed reason (as was the case with this decoration), and on my retirement the present young Duke invited my wife and myself, with my son and daughter-in-law, to have dinner with himself and the Duchess. It was a most auspicious occasion and, though touching, an enjoyable evening with a reception afterwards for all the keepers, loaders, dog men and police that went on until the small hours.

I must pay tribute to my wife, Eileen, who over so many long years has had so much to put up with, hardly ever knowing when I would be in for a meal, frequently with a lot of wet clothes to dry and hardly a day's outing, apart from a shopping visit to Chester. Such are the salt of the earth. My son, Malcolm, although always keen on the countryside, decided not to follow in my footsteps. He said plus fours would not look right on him as he's six foot three – what a poor excuse! I cannot blame him, and he has a good job, wife and family so there is much to be thankful for. God bless them all.

I think it would be impossible for me to pay adequate tribute to all the Grosvenors I have known, but to conclude I must make some attempt. Ever since coming to Eaton in 1929 I have always been treated most kindly, humanely and with appreciation by each Duke in turn. Always ready to realise no-one is perfect, they have all commiserated when there has been the odd failure. No-one really knows of the great generosity of the family as a whole, generosity which still continues today: it goes from the 2nd Duke's rebuilding of a school at Bosskop in Norway after the "scorched earth" policy when the Germans left at the end of the last war, to the magnificent gift that the present Duke gave me on my retirement. It is no wonder that such men inspire loyalty, and it may seem strange, but after long service you almost feel part of the family.

I could not wish to have had a more interesting, satisfying and gratifying job, nay, way of life. Maybe it is not the job to suit everyone, but with due dedication, because that is what it needs, work becomes a pleasure, and if you get pleasure from each day's work what more can you ask? May there always be a Duke of Westminster at Eaton, may the shooting always be good, and (I can't resist a cautionary word) may the environment improve and not deteriorate. That is all "the Crow" can say.